W9-CKB-100

Gifts from the
GARDEN

MADE FOR GIVING · MADE FOR GIVING · MADE FOR GIVING · MADE FOR GIVING

Gifts from the GARDEN

PAMELA
WESTLAND

Reader's
Digest

THE READER'S DIGEST ASSOCIATION, INC.
Pleasantville, New York • Montreal

A READER'S DIGEST BOOK
Conceived, edited, and designed by Marshall Editions

Copyright © 1998 Marshall Editions Developments Limited

All rights reserved. Unauthorized reproduction, in any
manner, is prohibited.

Library of Congress Cataloging in Publication Data

Westland, Pamela.
    Gifts from the garden / Pamela Westland.
        p.   cm. — (Made for giving)
    Includes index.
    ISBN 0-7621-0067-2
    1. Nature craft. 2. Gifts. 3. Dried flowers. 4. Dried foods.
5. Cookery (Fruit) 6. Wreaths.   I. Title II. Series
TT157.W4723 1998
745.5—dc21   97-40594

Reader's Digest and the Pegasus logo are registered trademarks
of The Reader's Digest Association, Inc.

Printed in Italy

PROJECT EDITOR   ESTHER LABI
PROJECT ART EDITOR   HELEN SPENCER
PHOTOGRAPHER   ANDREW SYDENHAM
STYLISTS   LABINA ISHAQUE, KATHERINE HARKNESS
FOOD ECONOMIST   BRIDGET SARGESON
HAND MODEL   MICHAELA MOHER
COPY EDITORS   GAIL DIXON SMITH, MAGGI MCCORMICK
DTP EDITORS   MARY PICKLES, LESLEY GILBERT
PRODUCTION EDITORS   EMMA DIXON, REBECCA CLUNES
MANAGING EDITOR   LINDSAY MCTEAGUE
EDITORIAL DIRECTOR   SOPHIE COLLINS
ART DIRECTOR   SEAN KEOGH
PRODUCTION   NIKKI INGRAM

Contents

INTRODUCTION

TENDING AND NURTURING A GARDEN, whether it is filled with fruits and vegetables or a profusion of flowers, is rewarding in itself, but it can be doubly so when you share the fruits of your labor with others.

THERE'S NOTHING QUITE LIKE a handmade gift, and on the following pages you will find comprehensive instructions on how to make and package personal yet professional-looking gifts, using flowers and produce from your own backyard. Of course, even if you don't have a garden, you can still buy everything you need from a flower shop, supermarket, or green grocer. You can pick or buy summer fruits and make jams and preserves to last through the winter, including the Orange and Apple Marmalade (pages 72–75) or Fruit Vinegars (pages 56–59), which are flavored with raspberries and blackberries. Alternatively, mark seasonal celebrations by making the springtime Mother's Day Posies (pages 28–31) or the colorful Midsummer Floral Wreath (pages 16–19) with whatever blooms your garden offers. If growing fruit and vegetables is your passion, there are some unusual wreaths and garlands to make, from the Vegetable Table Wreath (pages 108–111) and the Heart-shaped Harvest Wreath (pages 100–103) to the Garland of Dried Fruits (pages 96–99). Or simply use the tips and ideas on fresh and dried flowers, making preserves, and decorating wreaths at the beginning of every chapter as inspiration for creating your own gift.

ONCE YOU'VE MADE YOUR GIFT, enhance it by presenting it in a custom-made container. There are papier-mâché bowls, mini tote bags, and handmade envelopes to make, or buy some containers or boxes to decorate yourself. Finish your wrapped gift with a ribbon or bow and a handmade card. Whatever you choose to make, it is sure to be appreciated all the more by your family and friends for having been made by you.

Always follow one set of measurements – either imperial or metric – all the way through a recipe or project.

MAKING A RECTANGULAR BOX

Once you have learned how to make a rectangular box, vary the materials you use to create a satisfying variety of packages.

YOU WILL NEED

Cutting mat, craft knife, ruler, pencil, scissors

Two rectangular pieces of medium-weight cardboard (see sizing guide below)

Double-sided tape, 2 inches (5cm) wide

SIZING BOX BASE & LID

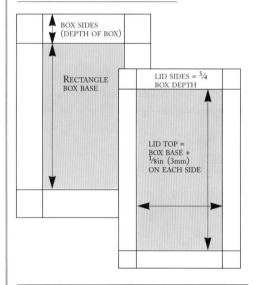

BOX SIDES (DEPTH OF BOX)

RECTANGLE BOX BASE

LID SIDES = ¾ BOX DEPTH

LID TOP = BOX BASE + ⅛in (3mm) ON EACH SIDE

Note

For a square box, use the basic principles outlined above but make the base a square. You can make your box of colored cardboard or make it out of acetate (see pages 82–83, steps 3–9).

TO MAKE A RECTANGULAR BOX *6"x 10½"x 2" (15 x 26 x 5cm)*

1 Place a piece of cardboard 14½ by 18¼ inches (36 by 46cm) on the cutting mat. Measure, draw, and cut a rectangle 10 by 14½ inches (25 by 36cm) for the base and sides of the box. Measure and draw a line 2 inches (5cm) in from and parallel to each side. This measurement is the depth of the box. The rectangle in the center, between the four lines, is the base.

4 Turn the cardboard over so the scored side is on the mat. Crease along all the scored lines and bring up the sides to form the depth of the box.

2 With a craft knife, score along all the pencil lines, but do not cut through the cardboard at this stage. To make the flaps that will form square corners, cut through one of the two pencil lines at each corner.

5 Peel off the backing from the tape at each corner in turn. With the sticky side inside, overlap the cut section and the side of the box and press the two thicknesses of cardboard together to make neat, square corners.

3 Measure and cut strips of double-sided tape to cover each of the squares at the corners. With the scored side of the cardboard still facing up, stick the tape onto each corner.

6 To make the lid, measure, draw, and cut out a rectangle 8¼ by 11 inches (20.5 by 27.5cm) from the remaining cardboard. Measure and draw a line 1 inch (2.5cm) in from and parallel to each of the four sides. This represents the side of the lid. Repeat steps 2 to 5 to finish the lid. ✽

EQUIPMENT

WORKING WITH FLOWERS, FRUITS, AND VEGETABLES is easy with a few basic items of equipment, available from craft stores, garden centers, and flower shops.

IF YOU ARE GOING TO CUT your own flowers, a sharp pair of pruning shears or floral scissors (used only for cutting flowers) is essential for gathering and trimming blooms. Floral wire, available from florists, is a dark gray-green wire that bends easily, yet holds its shape, and is perfect for making false stems for dried flowers or pinning bundles of decoration to wreath bases.

A VARIETY OF WREATH BASES, ranging from twig and raffia to floral foam, is available from craft stores and flower shops. Foam wreaths are particularly useful for dried and fresh floral arrangements. Gray foam bases are used dry, green ones are used wet.

YOU CAN BUY EVERYTHING YOU NEED for packaging your gifts at a craft store, including a cutting mat, craft knife, double-sided tape, and ruler. You will also find cardboard in many colors, wrapping paper, acetate, imitation silver leaf and gold-colored composition metal, paints, varnish, stencils, and ribbons – any of which will transform a simple gift into a masterpiece. With the right equipment, the art of creating an elegant and beautiful handmade gift is simple and easy. And with the following pages to inspire you, you can be as creative as you dare!

MAKING A ROUND BOX

A round box and lid is made of four pieces of cardboard – two circles and two thinner strips.

YOU WILL NEED

Cutting mat, craft knife, ruler, pencil, scissors

Piece of medium-weight cardboard for box base and top of lid (see Note below)

Piece of thinner cardboard for sides, as it bends into a neat circle (see Note below)

Drawing compass (or you can use a plate or other round item as a guide)

Packing tape, 2 inches (5cm) wide

Sheet of wrapping paper (see Note below)

Double-sided tape, 2 inches (5cm) wide

SIZING BOX BASE & LID   SIDES

1/4in (6mm)

DIAMETER OF LID

DIAMETER OF BOX BASE

1/4in (6mm)

LID = 1/2in (1.2cm) LARGER THAN BOX BASE (ADD 1/4in/6mm TO RADIUS)

CIRCUMFERENCE

BOX DEPTH

LID DEPTH = 1/2 BOX DEPTH

Note

Calculate how much you will need: Medium-weight cardboard width is equal to one diameter plus 1 inch (2.5cm); its length is twice the width. Thinner cardboard length is equal to the circumference of the lid; its width is the sum of the box and lid sides. Wrapping paper length is same as thinner cardboard; width is width of both cardboards plus 2 inches (5cm) for overlap.

TO MAKE A ROUND BOX *7 inches (18cm) in diameter and 2 inches (5cm) deep*

1 Place a piece of medium-weight cardboard 8 by 16 inches (20 by 40cm) on the cutting mat. For the box base, draw a 7-inch (18-cm) circle, using a compass or a round item as a guide. Cut out the circle with a craft knife. For the lid, draw and cut out a circle with a 7½ -inch (19-cm) diameter.

2 To make the side of the box, draw and cut a strip 2 by 23 inches (5 by 58cm) from a piece of thinner cardboard 3 by 24 inches (7.5 by 60cm). This strip is the depth of the box by the circumference plus 1 inch (2.5cm) for overlap. For the side of the lid cut a strip 1 by 23 inches (2.5 by 58cm).

3 To form the box base, cut about 36 strips of packing tape ½ inch (1.5cm) long and stick the ends around the rim of a bowl so they are close by. With the cardboard circle in your hand, stick the strips of tape close together around the edge, so half of each strip overlaps at the edge of the base.

4 Place the cardboard base on the work surface so the sticky side of the tape is uppermost. Place the strip for the side of the box upright against the edge of the base and, starting at one end of the strip, bend and stick the strips of packing tape to join the two together.

5 When you reach the other end of the cardboard strip, cut it so that the two ends butt up evenly, then cover the seam with a strip of packing tape. Make the lid in the same way as the box, following steps 3 and 4.

6 To cover the box with wrapping paper, follow the instructions on pages 34–35, steps 1–7. You will need a piece of paper about 12 by 24 inches (30 by 60cm). ✤

Fresh & Dried Flowers

As you gather each season's crop of bright and beautiful flowers, the makings of gifts to delight your friends are in your hands. Arrange spring flowers into fragrant posies clustered in a painted patchwork basket, make a colorful floral wreath to celebrate the summer, or show off your expertise with a tied bunch of parrot tulips presented in its own cellophane vase. For a gift that will last, plant a miniature garden in a stenciled pot, or for the avid bird lover, make a pair of seed wreaths and present them in a bright sunflower-patterned box.

Follow the guidelines for drying flowers and create gifts as the mood takes you: a dried flower posy, a fragrant pomander of dried rosebuds and seedheads, potpourri packed in an array of silk sachets, and a candle decorated with pressed flowers, set in its own presentation box.

Arranging Fresh Flowers

The steps you take to prepare freshly cut flowers and foliage before arranging them will enhance the pleasure they bring and make them last considerably longer.

Gathering flowers If you are cutting flowers from your garden in summer, gather them early in the morning or in the evening, never in the middle of the day. Cut the stems with floral scissors or pruning shears and, ideally, put them straight into a bucket of water.

Conditioning the blooms Once the flowers are indoors, strip off all the lower leaves and recut all the stems at an angle. Scrape away about 1 inch (2.5cm) of the bark from the end of woody stems, such as roses, and make a 2-inch (5-cm) slit in the stem. Stand the flowers and foliage in a bucket of cool but not ice-cold water in a cool place away from strong light for at least two hours, or preferably overnight, before arranging them. If you want to slow down the development of a small quantity of flowers, stand them in water in a refrigerator. By contrast, if you cut or buy flowers such as tulips and daffodils at the tight bud stage, when they are not showing any color, stand them in warm (not hot) water in a warm room for an hour or so until they begin to open.

Fresh flower maintenance To help your flowers and foliage stay fresh-looking for as long as possible, mix a solution of 1 tablespoon sugar and 1 teaspoon (5ml) regular strength household bleach to each pint (600ml) of water. Fill a vase with the solution, or soak floral foam or gel in it. As soon as you have completed an arrangement, spray it with a fine mist of cool water and leave it in a cool place away from strong light. If you are not presenting the gift immediately, spray the flowers twice a day to keep them fresh.

HOLDING MATERIALS

• Fresh flowers can be held in place with a number of materials, including marbles, gel, and floral foam in different shapes. You can fix foam to a dish by pressing a piece of green florist clay onto a plastic prong or frog. Press the frog on to the dish and push the foam onto the spikes.

• If the container for your floral arrangement is not waterproof, for example a basket, line it first with plastic. Then secure the foam by crisscrossing two strips of florist tape over the foam and onto the container.

PREPARING FLOWERS

● HOLLOW AND FLESHY flower stems, such as daffodils and delphiniums, should be recut under water. This helps to stop air locks from forming in the stems, which would prevent water moving up the stem.

● SAPPY STEMS SUCH AS spurge (*Euphorbia*) and poppies exude a white, latex-like substance. The stem of these flowers should be sealed by holding the end in the flame of a candle until the stem is singed black.

ARRANGING FLOWERS

1 Wet floral foam is ideal for a formal arrangement, as it holds flowers firmly in place and provides moisture for them, enabling your gift to last longer. Hide the foam with foliage, or some colored glass beads around the base.

3 Add feature flowers to outline the shape of the arrangement, then fill in the space. Make sure the feature flowers are evenly placed and the arrangement is pleasing from all the angles it may be viewed from.

2 Build up the shape of the arrangement with foliage or small, slightly pointed flowers, such as statice or lavender, which will form a background to the feature flowers. The shape can be triangular, domed, vertical, or horizontal.

4 Once you are satisfied with the final look of your arrangement, spray the flowers with a fine mist of water to keep them looking fresh. Leave the flowers in a cool place until you are ready to present your gift.

How To Dry Flowers

FOLLOW THESE SIMPLE TECHNIQUES and dry and store a wide range of flowers. You can then re-create the beauty of the garden for a gift at any time of the year.

HANGING FLOWERS The easiest method of drying small flowers, or flowers with tightly-clustered petals, such as rosebuds, is by hanging them upside down in bunches. Successful drying depends on the free circulation of warm dry air. Choose a position away from strong light, in a warm airy room. In general, the warmer the drying temperature, the shorter the drying time and the more pleasing the results will be. The temperature should never fall below 50°F (10°C). Hang the bunches so that they are not touching and leave them for several days. The exact time will depend on the moisture content of the flowers and the temperature and humidity of the room. The flowers are ready when the petals feel dry and crisp and the stems stiff.

DESICCANT DRYING Flowers with large petals, including roses that are fully opened, can also be dried with silica gel crystals, a desiccant available from florists. Using this method, flowers can be dried at room temperature, in an oven, or in a microwave. Choose an appropriate container: an airtight box with a lid, an ovenproof dish, or a microwave-safe dish respectively. Cover the flowers completely with silica gel (see right). To dry the flowers at room temperature, cover the container with a lid and check them after about 5 days. (Large flowers, such as peonies, may take up to 14 days to dry.) To dry them in an oven, place them in at the lowest setting, leave the door slightly open, and check after 20 minutes. In a microwave, dry flowers at the lowest power. The time will depend on the number of flowers, but check after about 4 minutes. Be careful not to overdry the flowers or they will crumble when you handle them. You can recycle the silica gel by spreading it on a baking tray and drying it in a low oven; store it in an airtight container.

USING A DESICCANT

1 Spread 1 inch (2.5cm) of silica gel in a container. Cut the flower stems to ½ inch (1.5cm) long and place them face upwards on the silica so they are not touching. Build up the silica to support the petals, sprinkle on crystals to fill the crevices, then cover them completely. Put in the microwave, oven, or leave at room temperature (see left).

2 When the flowers are dried, remove them from the silica gel crystals and brush off any residue. If you used the oven or microwave, let the flowers cool slightly before removing them from the dessicant since it gets quite hot.

AIR-DRYING FLOWERS

- PREPARE ALL PLANT materials as soon as possible after harvesting. Cut off any blemished flowers and strip off all the lower leaves. Use a craft knife to remove any discolored outer petals from otherwise perfect blooms.

- GATHER FLOWERS SUCH AS statice and roses into small bunches secured with a rubber band but leave larger flowers single. Hang the flowers on wire coathangers, or on string stretched across a room corner.

- HYDRANGEAS DRY BEST standing in a container with about 2 inches (5cm) of water. Stand the stems in the container so they are not touching and leave them away from strong light in a warm, airy room. The flowers dry as the water evaporates.

- HEAVY-HEADED FLOWERS such as mophead chrysanthemums and dahlias dry more successfully if the heads are supported upright. Slip the stems through the holes of a piece of chicken wire stretched over a wooden frame, or between wooden slats in a warm place. Leave them for several days.

ARRANGING DRIED FLOWERS

- SILICA-DRIED FLOWERS need false stems before being included in an arrangement. Bind floral wire to the short flower stems with silver wire. To make the stems look natural, bind them with florist tape, then arrange the flowers in a vase or dry floral foam.

- YOU CAN MAKE POTPOURRI using flowers which are air-dried in bunches, such as small spray roses and rosebuds, larkspur, and honeysuckle. Simply place the flower heads in a pretty bowl or cut the stems to ¾ inch (2cm) in length and arrange them on dry floral foam inside a painted box.

MIDSUMMER FLORAL WREATH

CAPTURE THE BEAUTY AND COLOR of some of the season's
loveliest flowers in this summery table wreath.

GIFT NEEDS

Floral scissors

Absorbent floral foam ring, 8 inches (20cm) in diameter

2–3 long stems of foliage such as ivy, geranium, or lady's mantle

12 pink roses

6 yellow roses

4 stems alstromeria (Peruvian lilies)

10 marigolds

About 20 stems bachlelor's buttons

Fine spray mister

PACKAGING NEEDS

Ruler, pencil, scissors, cutting mat, craft knife, string, paper towels, all-purpose glue

Wooden cheese box base, about 14 inches (35cm) in diameter

Fine-grit sandpaper (optional)

Soft cloth (optional)

White latex paint

½-inch (1.5-cm) paintbrush

Piece of paper, for the template

4 small foil containers, to use as palettes

Piece of white medium-weight cardboard

Cream, blue, and mauve water-based paints

Piece of synthetic household sponge, about 2 by 4 inches (5 by 10cm)

Tissue paper, to line box

Clear cellophane, about 1½ yards (1.5m) square

About 1½ yards (1.5m) each of two sheer ribbons

GIFT: Midsummer floral wreath

Put all the foliage and flowers in water and leave them in a cool place away from strong light until you are ready to arrange them.

1 Place the floral foam ring in water until it is saturated and does not float. Using floral scissors, cut the foliage and flower stems at a sharp angle, leaving about 4 inches (10cm) of stem. Return them to water.

2 Press the foliage sprays into the foam along the ring and also into the inner and outer rims, so that they conceal the base. Arrange the roses at intervals around the ring, pressing the stems into the foam at varying angles.

3 Position the alstromeria and marigolds around the ring, taking care to vary the height of the flowers to avoid giving the decoration a flat look. Place some of the flowers in the outer and inner rims of the foam to create a rounded effect.

4 Next add some of the bachelor's buttons in groups and a few of them individually, balancing their color throughout the design. ▶

5 Fill in any gaps with stems of foliage. Check that the base is not visible and that the wreath is pleasing from all angles.

6 Spray the ring with a fine mist of water and leave it in a cool place away from strong light until you are ready to package it. ▪

GIFTWRAP: Scalloped box

A shallow box sponge-painted in three colors is packaged in transparent paper and tied with sheer ribbons.

1 Sand the box if necessary and dust it with a soft cloth. Pour a little white paint into a foil container. Paint the inside of the box as well as the outside and leave it to dry.

3 Cut a strip of paper 3 inches (7.5cm) wide and half as long as the circumference. Fold the paper strip in half crosswise and half again, and then once more. Draw a shallow convex curve across the top of the folded paper and cut along the line through all the thicknesses with a pair of scissors.

2 Measure the circumference of the box using a piece of string. Cut a strip of cardboard 3 inches (7.5cm) wide and as long as the circumference, here 44 inches (110cm). You may have to cut two pieces and join them later.

4 Use the scalloped paper edge as a template and draw around it on the cardboard strip with a pencil. Cut around the outline with sharp scissors.

5 Pour some cream paint into a small container. Dip the sponge into the paint and wipe off any excess on paper towels. Sponge paint all over the cardboard so it is almost covered. Leave it to dry, then sponge the other side. Sponge the box, inside and out, in the same way. Wash the sponge.

6 Pour a little blue paint into a small container. Dip the sponge in water and squeeze it almost dry, then dip it in the paint, wiping off any excess on paper towels. Sponge the cardboard so some of the cream color shows through. Leave it to dry and sponge the other side. Sponge the box in the same way. Wash the sponge.

7 Pour a little mauve paint into a small container. Sponge the painted surfaces using the same technique as in step 6.

Note

Try making seasonal wreaths with different flowers, such as a winter floral wreath with mistletoe, ivy, and rosehips. Paint the box in toning colors of red, green, and blue.

8 Spread glue around the outside rim of the box and press the cardboard firmly onto it. Make neat seams if you are using two strips of cardboard. Set aside to let the glue dry.

9 Line the box with tissue paper and place the wreath on top. Position the box in the center of the cellophane and pull up the corners. Tie two ribbons in a bow around the cellophane and trim the ends. 🎁

PRESSED-FLOWER CANDLE

A CANDLE DECORATED WITH DRIED FLOWER PETALS AND LEAVES, and presented
on a bed of flowers, makes an attractive addition to any table or mantelpiece.

GIFT NEEDS

Scissors, hairdryer, heatproof bowl and saucepan, old spoon (optional)

2 sheets foolscap paper

Large candle, 3¾ inches (9.5cm) high and 2¾ inches (7cm) in diameter

Pressed petals, flowers, and leaves

Old candle or colorless wax

Wide paintbrush

PACKAGING NEEDS

Drawing compass (or a plate to use as a guide), pencil, cutting mat, craft knife, ruler, double-sided tape, scissors, felt-tip pen, floral scissors, glue (optional)

Piece of medium-weight cardboard, about 7 by 14 inches (18 by 36cm)

Piece of thinner cardboard, about 3 by 20 inches (8 by 50cm)

Piece of flat-finish gold wrapping paper, about 15 by 20 inches (38 by 50cm)

Double-sided tape, 2 inches (5cm) wide

Piece of acetate 5 by 19 inches (13 by 48cm)

Dry floral foam, to fit base of box

Gold marker pen

About 7 small dried rosebuds

About 5 dried safflower (Carthamus tinctorus) seed heads

4 sprays of fresh bay leaves

6 sprays of fresh rosemary

1 yard (1m) wire-edged ribbon, 4 inches (10cm) wide

1 yard (1m) wire-edged ribbon, 1 inch (2.5cm) wide, in a contrasting color

4 inches (10cm) fine silver wire, for making the bow

GIFT: Pressed-flower candle

1 To measure the area of the candle to decorate, wrap a piece of paper around the candle and then use scissors to trim it to the correct height and width of the candle.

2 So that you can work quickly when you start to decorate the candle, arrange the dried petals and other pressed flowers and leaves on the piece of paper until you have a design you find pleasing.

3 Heat the surface of the candle one section at a time with a hairdryer to melt the wax slightly and make it sticky. Gently press the dried flowers onto the surface with your fingertips.

4 Wrap a sheet of paper around the candle and roll it on the work surface to make sure the flowers and leaves are well attached. Continue heating and decorating one section at a time, until the design is complete. ▶

5 Place the old candle or colorless wax in a small heatproof bowl over a saucepan of simmering water. Heat until the wax melts.

6 Dip the paintbrush in the melted wax and, working quickly so the wax does not solidify, brush over the flowers to seal them. Let the wax dry completely, about 10 minutes, before touching the surface. ▪

GIFTWRAP: Bed of roses

Lift the lid off this glittering see-through package and you have a ready-made centerpiece, complete with candle, to add a festive touch to any dinner table.

1 To make the base and lid, cut two 6-inch (15-cm) circles from the medium-weight cardboard and two strips 1 by 19 inches (2.5 by 48cm) from the thinner cardboard. Follow the instructions for making a round box on pages 8 and 9.

2 To cover the lid, cut a circle of wrapping paper to fit the top and a strip 1½ by 19 inches (4 by 48cm) for the side. Cover the back of the strip with double-sided tape and place the lid in the middle. Peel off the backing from the tape and press the lid down firmly.

3 Snip the overlapping paper at intervals around the edges with scissors, to make folding easier. Fold over the two edges and press in place on the inside and top of the lid.

4 Cover the back of the paper circle with double-sided tape; trim the edge with scissors. Peel off the backing and stick the circle to the lid. Cover the base of the box in the same way.

5 Stick double-sided tape around the perimeter of the inside of the lid. Ease the acetate widthwise into the lid to form a cylinder and secure the ½-inch (1.5-cm) overlap top and bottom with double-sided tape.

6 Cut the floral foam to fit the box base. Stand the candle in the center of the foam and draw around it. Cut out the circle with a craft knife and fit the foam into the box base. Press the candle into the hole.

7 Highlight the rose petal edges with a gold marker pen to reflect the candlelight. Be careful – the petals can be fragile. Trim the roses and safflower stems with floral scissors to 2 inches (5cm).

8 To decorate the box, arrange a ring of bay leaves and short sprigs of rosemary around the base of the candle, sticking the stems in the foam. Then arrange the small roses and carthamus among the foliage. Add more flowers or leaves to cover any gaps if the foam is visible.

9 Ease the acetate cylinder and lid into the box. To make a bow, place two ribbons together and make five concertina folds. Tie the ends together with a piece of wire. Ease out the folds to form three loops. Stick the bow to the top of the package with double-sided tape or a drop of glue. 🎁

A MINIATURE GARDEN

GIVE YOUR FRIENDS THE JOY OF WATCHING THE GARDEN BLOOM with an indoor
bulb garden, planted in a stencilled terra-cotta pot and presented in a woven basket.

GIFT NEEDS

Pencil, tracing paper, cutting mat, craft knife, string, pen, piece of chalk, masking tape

Round terra-cotta pot, about 8¹⁄₂ inches (21.5cm) in diameter and 4¹⁄₂ inches (11.5cm) deep, with drainage hole

Green dry-brush stencil paint and stencil brush

Few pieces of broken flowerpot (known as crocks)

About 3 tablespoons gravel

About 1 pound (500g) soiless potting mix

About 10 miniature narcissus bulbs

About 10 miniature daffodil bulbs

About 8 dwarf tulip bulbs

About 20 grape hyacinth bulbs

Small craft brush

Fine spray mister

PACKAGING NEEDS

Pen, masking tape

1 yard (1m) sheer beige ribbon, 2³⁄₄ inches (7cm) wide

Sheet of plain paper

Green dry-brush stencil paint and stencil brush

Basket about 10 inches (25cm) in diameter and 6 inches (15cm) deep

Piece of plastic sheet (optional)

Plant saucer, to fit in basket,

Dry sphagnum moss

2–3 stems ivy

Piece of cardboard 3 by 4 inches (7.5 by 10cm) for the label (see Note)

6 inches (15cm) narrow cane (see Note)

GIFT: A miniature garden

Make sure the terra-cotta pot has a drainage hole in the bottom.

1 To decorate the pot, trace the stencil outline on page 26 onto tracing paper and cut out the outline using a craft knife.

2 Measure around the center of the circumference of the pot with a piece of string. Figure out how many stencil outlines will fit, and the distance to leave between each one. Mark these points on the string with pen. Hold the string around the pot again and repeat the marks on the pot with chalk.

3 Place the stencil on the first chalk mark and secure it with masking tape. If you turn the pot upside-down, make sure the stencil is, too. Using circular brush strokes, paint over the stencil with green paint.

4 Reposition and secure the stencil on the next chalk mark, taking care not to smudge the paint. Stencil the pattern and repeat around the pot. ▶

5 Scatter the pieces of broken flowerpot in the terra-cotta pot to cover the drainage hole, and scatter the gravel over them. Turn the pot around so that a stencil is centered at the front.

6 Half-fill the pot with potting mix and pack it down. Press the narcissus bulbs in a semicircle row into the potting mix at the back and sides of the pot. Plant the tulip bulbs in front of the narcissus, in the center of the pot, but leave room at the front for more bulbs.

7 Plant a semicircle of daffodils in front of the tulips, joining up with the narcissus at the sides. Finally, plant the grape hyacinth bulbs in a semicircle cluster around the front of the pot. The tops of the bulbs should be about $3\frac{1}{4}$ inches (8cm) below the rim of the pot.

8 Pack some potting mix around each bulb, then add more to a level of $\frac{3}{4}$ inch (2cm) below the rim. Brush away any potting mix clinging to the side of the pot and leaves. Spray the bulbs with water so that the potting mix is moist but not wet and soggy. ▪▪

GIFTWRAP: Stenciled ribbon

A ribbon with a continuous stenciled pattern repeats the motif decorating the terra-cotta planter.

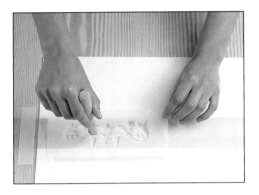

1 Place the ribbon on a piece of paper on the work surface, pull it taut, and secure it with masking tape. Secure the stencil at one end of the ribbon with masking tape. Dab the stencil brush in green paint and fill in the outline using circular strokes.

2 Move the stencil along the ribbon, leaving about 2 inches (5cm) between repeats. Secure and color the design as before. Continue until you have decorated all the ribbon.

3 If the basket is loosely woven, line it with a piece of plastic. Put the plant saucer in bottom of the basket and add dry sphagnum moss around the sides. Place the planted terra-cotta pot on top.

4 Tie the stencilled ribbon in a bow. Decorate the basket handle with ivy and tie the bow to the basket. Trim the ends of the ribbon neatly. ✽

Note

If you wish, make a label from a piece of cardboard and copy the plant care instructions onto it. Make a slit in a piece of cane, push the cardboard into it and press the cane into the bowl. Plant care instructions: "Keep the soil moist but never wet. Cut off flowers as they fade. After they have flowered, plant the bulbs in a windowbox or garden to flower the following year. Let the leaves die before cutting them off."

MOTHER'S DAY POSIES

A PAINTED SLATTED BASKET FILLED WITH SMALL POSIES of primroses,
violets, and grape hyacinths will delight any mother or grandmother.

GIFT NEEDS

Rubber bands, scissors

2 bunches violets

2 bunches primroses

1 bunch grape hyacinths

About 16 ivy, primrose, or violet leaves

Floral scissors

About 32 inches (80cm) each satin ribbons, ⅛ inch (3mm) wide in yellow, blue, and mauve

Makes 4 posies

PACKAGING NEEDS

Slatted wooden basket 4½ by 7 inches (11.5 by 18cm), lined with plastic sheet (see Step 7)

Fine-grit sandpaper

Soft cloth

Water-based acrylic paints in cream, mauve, green, purple, blue, and yellow

Small paintbrush

6 small foil containers, to use as palettes

Fine-pointed craft paintbrush

Double-sided tape (optional, see Step 7)

¾ yard (70cm) each purple and mauve satin ribbon, ½ inch (1.5cm) wide

Dry sphagnum moss

GIFT: Mother's day posies

Put the flowers and leaves in water, spray them with a fine mist of water, and leave them in a cool place away from strong light until you are ready to use them.

1 Untie the bunches of flowers and spread them out on the work surface so that they are in easy reach. Cut the yellow, blue, and mauve ribbons into 8-inch (20-cm) lengths.

2 To make the first posy, pick up violets one by one and gather them loosely in one hand. Ease out the flower heads gently so that they are not crushed together.

3 Arrange a ring of primroses around the bunch, with the flowers slightly lower than the violets. Avoid packing the flowers too close together.

4 Arrange an outer ring of violets around the primroses, then add a ring of leaves. These protect the flowers as well as being decorative. ▶

5 Secure the posy with a rubber band, then tie around it with two or three of the ribbons together. Trim the stems to the same length.

6 Make more posies in the same way, varying the combination of flowers, perhaps with primroses and grape hyacinths together, or all three types of flowers. The basket shown here will hold about four small posies. Put the posies in water until you pack them. ■■

GIFTWRAP: Patchwork basket

When the little posies have become just a fond memory, the cheerfully colorful basket can be used as a sewing or knitting holdall.

1 Lightly sand the basket, especially around the rim and the handle. Then dust it with a soft cloth.

2 Pour a little cream paint into a small container. Paint the handle and the rim of the basket and leave it to dry. Apply a second coat of paint.

3 Pour the other paints into separate containers. Dab a spot of color onto each slat to indicate the color it is to be painted. You can use the different colors at random or in a more formal pattern. Wash the brush between colors.

4 Paint the squares that are to be in the first color, here mauve. Leave the paint to dry. For a good finish, apply a second coat and leave to dry.

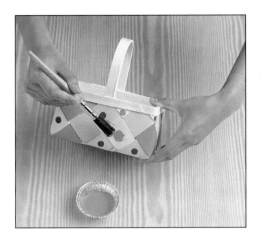

5 Next, paint the squares that are to be in the second color, here green. Leave the basket to dry. As before, apply a second coat. When the green paint is dry, paint the remaining squares in purple and blue, letting the paint dry between colors and coats.

6 When all the paint is dry, use a fine-pointed paintbrush to decorate some of the squares. With the yellow paint, dab polka dots on some of the green squares. If you like, when the dots are dry, you can paint over them with diluted green paint to achieve a subtle raised-dot effect.

7 Use the fine-pointed paintbrush to go over any unevenly painted edges or to overpaint any slight spills. If the basket you use is not already lined, cut a piece of plastic to fit and attach it inside, just below the rim, with double-sided tape.

8 Tie the two satin ribbons in a small bow around one side of the basket handle and trim the ends neatly.

9 Line the basket with moss. When you are ready to present your gift, gently dry the stems of the posies and arrange them in the basket. ❦

Note

As a variation, you might like to use grape hyacinths and dwarf daffodils in place of the violets and primroses. Tied with raffia, the posy assumes a less formal look.

BIRDSEED WREATHS

A PAIR OF HANGING BIRDSEED WREATHS packed in a sunny
sunflower box will give pleasure to birds and bird-lovers alike.

GIFT NEEDS

Kitchen tongs, large spoon

*About 1 pound (500g) birdseed, using seeds
gathered from the garden or from a petstore*

Wide, shallow dish

Wide, deep saucepan

8 ounces (250g) shortening

½ cup (125g) cornmeal

½ cup (125g) peanut butter

*2 natural straw or twig wreath forms,
8 inches (20cm) and 6 inches (15cm)
in diameter*

*2 ½ yards (2.5m) green grosgrain ribbon,
1 inch (2.5cm) wide*

*1 yard (90cm) yellow grosgrain ribbon,
1 inch (2.5cm) wide*

PACKAGING NEEDS

*String, ruler, pencil, scissors,
all-purpose glue*

*Round box with lid, at least 9 inches (23cm)
in diameter and 5 inches (12.5cm) deep*

*2–3 sheets of wrapping paper with
sunflower pattern*

Double-sided tape, 2 inches (5cm) wide

*14 inches (35cm) green grosgrain ribbon,
1 ½ inches (4cm) wide, for handles*

Small plastic bag

Tissue paper, for packing

GIFT: Birdseed wreaths

1 Place the birdseed in a shallow bowl. Melt the shortening in a saucepan, add the cornmeal and peanut butter, and stir over low heat until the mixture has blended. Turn off the heat and let the mixture cool slightly.

2 Pick up one of the wreaths with tongs. Dip the wreath in the melted fat mixture, spooning it over the inside of the wreath so that all the surfaces are covered.

3 Using the tongs, transfer the wreath to the shallow dish of birdseed. Press the wreath into the bowl of birdseed to cover one side with as much seed as possible.

4 Turn the wreath over, press it firmly into the seed, and spoon more seed over the wreath to cover all sides. Spoon on more fat and more seed to cover any bare patches. Build up several layers of fat and seed, and cover the other wreath in the same way, reheating the fat mixture if necessary. Refrigerate both wreaths overnight. ►

5 Cut two 18-inch (45-cm) lengths from each of the ribbons. Loop a pair of coordinated ribbons around each of the seed-covered wreaths. The recipient can tie the ends to make a hanging loop of the right length.

6 Cut the remaining green ribbon in half and thread each piece through the loop around the wreath. Tie it in a bow to decorate the top of the wreath. Trim the ribbon ends. ▪▪

GIFTWRAP: A burst of sunflowers

A deep cardboard box covered with bright floral wrapping paper and given decorative ribbon handles will make a useful container for the kitchen, too.

1 To work out how much wrapping paper you need to cover the box, measure the circumference of the lid and the box using string; measure the sides with a ruler. The paper needs to be as long as the circumference plus ½ inch (1.5cm) overlap and as wide as the depth plus 1 inch (2.5cm).

3 To cover the box base and lid, draw around them on the paper and cut out the circles using scissors.

2 Place the wrapping paper on the work surface. Measure and cut two strips for the inside and the side of the box, and one for the side of the lid.

4 Cover the back of the strips and circles of paper with double-sided tape, allowing the tape to overlap the edges where necessary. Using scissors, trim the tape to fit exactly.

5 Peel the backing paper off the tape on the larger strip of wrapping paper. Position the box on its side in the center of the paper and carefully smooth the paper around it.

6 Using scissors, snip into the paper overlapping the edges at ½-inch (1.5-cm) intervals, to make them easier to stick down. Fold the edges onto the base of the box and then inside the rim. Cover the inside of the box.

7 Remove the backing paper from the paper circle for the base of the box. Press it in position, smoothing it out carefully as you go. Cover the side then the top of the lid in the same way.

8 To make the handles, cut the ribbon in half crosswise. Turn over ¼ inch (6mm) to the wrong side at each end. Glue the folds down. Then fold each piece of ribbon in half with the folds inside and glue the two folds together. Glue one handle to each side of the lid.

9 Fill the plastic bag with birdseed and seal the top. Use cutout flowers or strips of wrapping paper to decorate the bag. Pack the wreaths and the bag of birdseed in the box between layers of crumpled tissue paper. ✿

Note

The two birdseed wreaths are packed with a bag of seed, so the recipient can replenish the wreaths from time to time.

HAND-TIED TULIPS

TWO-TONE PARROT TULIPS in a striking red and purple color combination are gathered in a dramatic hand-tied bunch and presented in their own cellophane "vase."

GIFT NEEDS

Floral scissors or craft knife, scissors, bucket of water

About 15 red and purple parrot tulips

6–10 red tulips

6–10 mauve tulips

3–4 stems small-leaf variegated ivy

1½ yards (1.5m) raffia

½ yard (45cm) purple satin ribbon, 1 inch (2.5cm) wide

Fine mist sprayer

PACKAGING NEEDS

1 yard (1m) square clear cellophane

1½ yards (1.5m) each of red and purple sheer ribbons, 1½ inches (4cm) wide

Watering can with narrow spout

GIFT: Hand-tied tulips

Put the tulips in a bucket of cold water away from strong light until you are ready to arrange them.

1 As soon as you bring the tulips indoors, strip off the lower leaves, and cut the stems at an angle, leaving enough of the stem to allow for a further trim in Step 8. Return them to water.

2 To compose the bunch, hold one of the parrot tulips by the stem. Place another one across it about half way down the stem so that the flower is angled diagonally to the left.

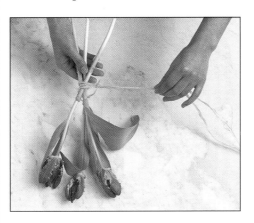

3 Add another parrot tulip, this time with the head angled diagonally to the right. Loop the raffia around the stems where they cross and pull it taut.

4 Turn the bunch one half-turn and add two more parrot tulips, each angled diagonally in opposite directions. Bind the raffia once around the stems to hold them in place. ▶

5 Continue turning the bunch one half-turn and adding single-color tulips as well as parrot tulips in pairs in this way. Bind once around the stems every two or three turns.

6 When all the parrot tulips and the single-color tulips have been used, add some long stems of ivy to "frame" the arrangement.

7 Bind the raffia around all the stems several times, then tie it in a knot and cut off the ends.

8 Using floral scissors, cut the stems straight across the bottom so that the bunch can stand up.

9 Tie the ribbon around the stems to cover the raffia, make a double knot and cut off the ends.

10 To stop the tulips from opening, spray the flowers with a fine mist of cold water and stand them in a bucket of water in a cool place and away from strong light until you are ready to wrap them. ▪

GIFTWRAP: See-through vase

The hand-tied tulips are presented in a cellophane wrapping, which forms a clear vase that can be filled with water. This practical aspect is sure to be appreciated by a busy hostess.

1 Place the cellophane on a work surface in a diamond shape, and lay the flowers in the middle. Bring the bottom point up and over the flowers to meet the point at the top. Pull out the side points so the cellophane is taut.

2 Fold the two side points inward, gather the cellophane around the middle of the stems, and tie around them tightly with raffia.

3 Hold the two ribbons together and knot them around the bunch. Tie a double bow and trim the ends neatly with scissors.

Note

For a different look, try wrapping the hand-tied bunch of tulips in two sheets of colored cellophane, such as red and purple, and tying it with a sheer gold ribbon.

4 Pull down the four points of the cellophane so that they form a collar around the flowers.

5 Using the watering can, carefully pour water into the cellophane vase. When transporting the flowers, stand them in their cellophane vase in a bucket to avoid spilling the water. 🎁

Dried Flower Posy

This flat-backed posy of summer flowers can be hung on a wall
or door, or laid on a bedroom or living room table.

GIFT NEEDS

Scissors, floral scissors

About 2 feet (60cm) raffia

5 stems dried rose leaves, perhaps saved from the Rosebud and Seed Head Pomander (page 45)

About 30 stems dried wheat

About 9 stems dried pink larkspur

About 9 stems dried blue larkspur

About 6 stems yellow achillea

5-7 dried red roses

3 dried peonies

About 6 stems dried white "pearl everlasting" (Matricaria)

24 inches (60cm) satin ribbon, 1½ inches (4cm) wide

PACKAGING NEEDS

Ruler, pencil, craft knife, cutting mat, scissors

Piece of medium-weight cardboard 19½ by 27 inches (49.5 by 70cm) for the box base

Double-sided tape, 2 inches (5cm) wide

Piece of medium-weight cardboard 13 by 21 inches (33.5 by 54cm) for the lid

Piece of acetate 7 by 15 inches (18 by 38cm), for the "window"

4 yards (3.5m) wire-edged ribbon, 3 inches (7.5cm) wide

About ¾ yard (70cm) square of cellophane

Tissue paper

GIFT: Dried flower posy

1 Cut the raffia in half. Using floral scissors, cut the stems of rose leaves to about 16 inches (40cm) long and place them across one of the lengths of raffia, which will later be tied around all the stems.

2 Arrange the wheat stems on top of the rose leaves, with the longest, about 18 inches (45cm), in the center and shorter ones making a narrow fan shape at the sides.

3 Trim off any side shoots of the pink and blue larkspur stems with floral scissors. Arrange the stems on the wheat, with the longest at the center of the bunch and shorter ones at the sides.

4 Add the yellow achillea and arrange the roses through the center of the bunch. Cut some stems short so the flowers come about two-thirds of the way down the length of the posy. ▶

5 Arrange the three peonies and the pearl everlasting at the center of the bunch. Wind the raffia around the stems and secure with a double knot. Trim the ends of the stems into a V-shape with scissors.

6 Double the remaining length of raffia, thread it through the raffia at the back of the bunch, and knot it to make a hanging loop. Tie the ribbon in a bow to hide the raffia and neaten the ends with scissors. ▪▪

GIFTWRAP: Window box

The pink presentation box has a transparent lid that shows off the country-garden posy to perfection.

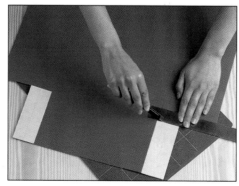

1 To make the box base, use a pencil to draw lines 5 inches (12.5cm) in from each edge of the larger piece of cardboard. Lightly score the lines with a craft knife. Be careful not to cut all the way through.

2 On the short sides, measure 3 inches (7.5cm) in from each corner. Draw a line 5 inches (12.5cm) long parallel to the edge and cut these corner sections away with a craft knife.

3 Cut four pieces of double-sided tape 5 inches (12.5cm) long and stick the tape on the rectangular flaps at the corners. Using a craft knife, make a cut through the short side of each flap.

4 Fold along all the scored lines. Making one corner at a time, remove the backing paper from the tape, fold up the sides, and press the flaps to make neat corners.

5 To make the lid, draw a line 1½ inches (4cm) in from each edge of the smaller piece of cardboard. Lightly score along the lines, then cut through one of the lines at each corner section with a craft knife, as in Step 3. Apply double-sided tape to each corner flap, trimming the tape to fit.

6 To make a "window," draw a line 3 inches (7.5cm) in from each edge of the cardboard and cut out the central rectangle with a craft knife.

7 Fold along all the scored lines. Remove the backing strips from the double-sided tape and fold the corner flaps in where they overlap the sides of the box. Stick double-sided tape to the cardboard inner edges of the window and peel off the backing strips. Press down the acetate into the window of the lid.

8 Cut eight 1-inch (2.5-cm) pieces of double-sided tape and stick them on either side of each corner of the box, about 1 inch (2.5cm) from the base. Peel the backing strips from the tape. Place the center of the ribbon at the back of the box and wrap it around the box to the front, pulling it taut and pressing it onto the strips of tape.

9 Tie the ribbon in a bow at the front of the box and trim the ends with scissors. Crumple cellophane and tissue paper in the box before putting in the posy. �

ROSEBUD AND SEED HEAD POMANDER

A SWEETLY SCENTED hanging decoration studded with roses
brings a touch of summer into the home all year round.

GIFT NEEDS

Floral scissors, scissors, all-purpose glue (optional), pencil

2 floral pins or 8 inches (20cm) flexible wire cut in half with wire cutters and each bent into a U shape

Dry floral foam ball 2½ inches (6.5cm) in diameter

10 inches (25cm) satin ribbon, ⅛ inch (3mm) wide

About 16 small dried poppy seed heads

Gold craft paste

Small craft paintbrush

About 36 small dried pink rosebuds

About 24 small dried yellow rosebuds

About 16 small dried love-in-a-mist seed heads

1½ yards (1.5m) sheer floral-patterned ribbon, 1½ inches (4cm) wide

PACKAGING NEEDS

Scissors, all-purpose glue, double-sided tape

Round wooden, cardboard or papier-mâché box, at least 6 inches (15cm) in diameter and 5 inches (12.5cm) deep

Pink and yellow water-based paints

2 small foil containers, to use as palettes

Small piece synthetic household sponge

1 sheet of floral-patterned wrapping paper

Clear water-based flat varnish

Small paintbrush

1 yard (1m) metallic ribbon, 2 inches (5cm) wide

Tissue paper, for packing

Dried rose petals, for packing (optional)

GIFT: Rosebud and seed head pomander

1 Press one of the floral pins or U-shaped wires into the foam ball, leaving a small loop extending above the foam. Thread the narrow ribbon through the floral pin and knot the two ends together. Push the wire right into the foam.

2 Brush the tops of the poppy seed heads with a little gold craft paste to give them a slight sparkle. Leave the seed heads to dry.

3 Using floral scissors, cut the stems off the seed heads and roses, leaving about 1 inch (2.5cm) of stem to stick into the foam ball.

4 Press the stem of one of the pink roses close to the floral pin. Then arrange a ring of pink roses all around the ball, pressing them in close together so there are no gaps. ▶

5 On one side of the ring of roses, add a ring of poppy seed heads. Try to place each seed head between two roses in the adjacent ring, but position them so there are no gaps. If the poppy seed heads spring out of the foam, you may need to glue them in place.

6 Arrange a ring of yellow roses next to the poppy seed heads, positioning each flower between two of the seed heads in the previous ring as before. Complete that side of the ball with another ring of pink roses, adding more pink roses to fill in the center so the foam is completely covered.

7 Turn the flower ball over and arrange a ring of love-in-a-mist seed heads close to the first ring of pink roses. Complete the ball with yellow and pink roses, as described in Step 6.

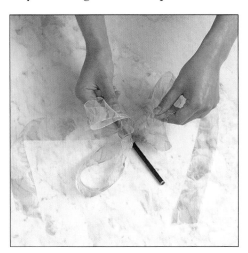

8 To decorate the pomander, tie the sheer ribbon around a pencil in a bow with loops about 4 inches (10cm) long. Tie the ends of the ribbon into another bow and trim the ends with scissors. Slip the bow off the pencil.

9 Thread the second floral pin or U-shaped wire through the center of the bow and press it firmly into the foam ball close to the hanging loop. ▪▪

GIFTWRAP: Miniature hatbox

A marbled pink and golden yellow box is decorated with decoupage flowers and a glittering ribbon band.

1 Pour a little pink paint into a small container. Using the sponge, dab the paint over the box and lid, and leave to dry. Sponge on a second coat if necessary and leave it to dry. Wash the sponge thoroughly after each coat.

2 Pour a little yellow paint into a small container and sponge the color sparsely over the pink to create a marbled effect. Leave it to dry.

3 To make the decoupage, cut out a selection of flowers and leaves from the wrapping paper with scissors. It may be easier to roughly cut out each shape first, so you have a smaller piece of paper to handle.

4 Glue the cutout shapes around the side of the box close to the base. When the glue is dry, varnish the box and lid, and leave to dry. Apply another coat of varnish and leave to dry.

5 Cut a strip of ribbon to wrap over the top and sides of the lid. Pull the ribbon taut over the lid and stick the ends inside the lid with double-sided tape. Tie a bow with the remaining ribbon. Tie a second bow using the ends of the first.

6 Finish the ends of the bow with scissors and glue it to the ribbon on the lid. Line the box with tissue paper and scatter a few rose petals inside before putting in the pomander. 🎁

SCENTED SACHETS

SILK SACHETS FILLED WITH A TRADITIONAL BLEND of rose petals and lavender
make delightful token gifts or accompaniments for a thank-you note or get-well card.

GIFT NEEDS

Baking sheet, lidded jar

FOR THE POTPOURRI

2 cups fresh rose petals

2 cups fresh lavender flowers

1 cup fresh chamomile flowers

3 tablespoons fresh rosemary leaves

About 16 fresh bay leaves

2 teaspoons ground cinnamon

3-4 drops rose oil or lavender oil

Makes enough for about six sachets

FOR SIX SACHETS

Ruler, pencil, scissors, iron, needle and thread, tracing paper

6 pieces of silk or other closely woven fabric 4¹/₂ by 9 inches (11.5 by 23cm) for flat sachets and 4¹/₂ by 11 inches (11.5 by 28cm) for the bag sachets

Double-sided tape, 2 inches (5 cm) wide

Selection of 6 coordinated ribbons or scraps of coordinated fabric to decorate the sachets

PACKAGING NEEDS

Ruler, pencil, all-purpose glue

6 sheets handmade paper 8 by 11¹/₂ inches (20 by 29cm)

Double-sided tape, ¹/₂ inch (1.2cm) wide

Selection of 6 coordinated ribbons or scraps of coordinated fabric to decorate the envelopes

GIFT: Scented sachets

The instructions to make the potpourri are given for using fresh flowers and herbs. If you already have dried ones, begin at Step 2.

1 Spread the rose petals, lavender, chamomile flowers, rosemary, and bay leaves on a baking sheet, keeping the flowers and herbs separate. Leave the tray in a warm place away from strong light for 2 to 3 days until the leaves and flowers feel dry and crisp.

2 Lightly crumble the herbs and put them in a bowl with the flowers. Add the ground cinnamon and rose or lavender oil to the flowers and herbs and stir until the mixture is well blended.

3 Put the potpourri into a jar, close the lid, and leave for about two weeks. Stir or shake the jar every day if possible, to help the contents infuse.

4 To make each sachet pillow, use a piece of fabric 4¹/₂ by 9 inches (11.5 by 23cm). With a warm iron, press a ¹/₄-inch (6-mm) single hem to the wrong side on all four edges. ▶

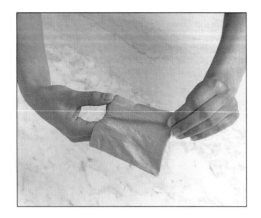

5 Fold the piece of silk in half with the right sides together. Using a needle and thread, sew the sides of the sachet together and half of the top, leaving a gap for adding the potpourri, and turn right side out. Make the other sachet pillows the same way.

6 To decorate a sachet with a heart, trace the heart below on a piece of paper and cut it out to make a template. Stick a piece of double-sided tape to the wrong side of a scrap of fabric, draw around the heart template, and cut out the shape. Remove the backing strip and stick the heart to the sachet. Decorate the other sachets with hearts or sew on ribbon bows.

7 Spoon the potpourri into the sachets until they are two-thirds full. Sew up the opening and, if you wish, sew in a loop for hanging or tie a ribbon right around the sachet.

8 To make a bag sachet, use a piece of fabric 4½ by 11 inches (11.5 by 28cm). Using a warm iron, press ¼ inch (6mm) to the wrong side on the long sides and 1 inch (2.5cm) on the short sides. Hem the 1-inch (2.5-cm) turns then, with the right sides together, sew the two long sides.

9 Turn the bag inside out. Place the potpourri in the bag to about two-thirds full. Tie a ribbon around the neck of the bag. ▪▪

GIFTWRAP: Handmade-paper envelopes

Contrast the silky smooth sachets with rough handmade paper. The aroma wafting through the envelope provides a gift for the senses.

1 Measure 2½ inches (6cm) from the top of each sheet of paper and fold up the bottom to this point. Mark the center of the top edge with a pencil. Measure 2 inches (5cm) from the top on each side and draw lines from these marks to the center mark with a pencil.

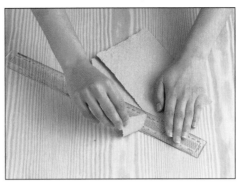

2 To make the envelope flap, place a ruler along a line and tear off the corner of the paper, holding the ruler firmly. Repeat on the other side.

3 Cut two strips of double-sided tape 4 inches (10cm) long and stick them to the sides above the fold in the paper. Fold up the bottom section and press the sides onto the tape.

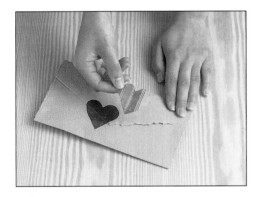

4 Make two heart shapes from scraps of fabric as before. Place the sachet in the envelope and close the flap. Remove the backing strips from the hearts and place over the flap.

5 Another way to decorate the envelope is to wrap a ribbon around it, joining the two ends with double-sided tape under the flap. Secure the flap with a small piece of double-sided tape, make a bow, and glue it to the flap. 🎁

Note

Try trimming the envelopes in different ways. Spread thin lines of glue around the edges of the flap, and press on narrow ribbon, or tie a ribbon right around the envelope. You could also try using different types of paper, such as marbled paper.

Garden Delicacies

❦ MAKING A BATCH OF PRESERVES is one of the most thoughtful ways to share a fruit and vegetable harvest with friends. Transform fresh fruit into scented rose-petal jelly or a trio of berry sauces. Make squares of apple sweetmeats and pack them in a box stenciled with gilded apples or turn the summer's supply of apricots into a delicious spread, presented in a stucco-effect box. Apple and orange marmalade, with a hint of cilantro and a bright decoupage canister, will spice up any breakfast, and blueberry molds, in a berry-colored tote bag, will provide the perfect accompaniment to meat later in the day.

There are spicy recipes, too, including chow-chow relish, in a colorful string-covered container, and the ever-popular corn and pepper relish, nestling in an aromatic herb basket. The easy-to-make fruit vinegars, presented in a stamped bag, are sure to add piquancy to many of your friends' favorite dishes.

JAMS AND PRESERVES

JARS OF HOMEMADE PRESERVES and jellies make welcome gifts all year round. Build up a stock of presents, season after season.

SETTING AGENTS For a preserve to set, it must contain enough pectin, acid, and sugar. Fruits that are high in both pectin and acid, and thus give a good set, include apples, lemons, limes, bitter oranges, red currants, and black currants. Fruits that are low in acid and pectin, such as strawberries, pears, cherries, and rhubarb, may be combined with high-pectin fruit or lemon juice to set the preserve. Commercial pectin, which is available as a liquid or powder, can also be added to a preserve to help it set. To hasten the dissolving process and minimize the temperature loss of the preserve, sugar should be warmed in a preheated oven, set to 250°F (130°C), for about 15 to 20 minutes before adding it to the preserve. Stir the sugar into the preserve over low heat, until the sugar has dissolved.

EQUIPMENT You can buy most of the equipment you need, including jelly bags, canning jars, large, deep saucepans or kettles, and preserving pans, from a kitchen supply store. When you are making sugar-based preserves, choose a large saucepan with a heavy base, which will ensure an even distribution of heat and help prevent burning. Preserving pans, which are usually made of copper, brass, enamel, or aluminum, are wider at the top than the base. This allows for maximum evaporation of the preserve. Unlined brass, copper, or aluminum pans, and iron or galvanized pans, are not suitable for vinegar-based preserves; instead, choose one made of enamel, glass, or stainless steel, or lined with tin or a non-stick coating. Take care not to fill your pan more than halfway, to leave room for the preserve to boil safely.

STERILIZING JARS

1 Check that the glass is not chipped or cracked. Wash the jars and lids and rinse them thoroughly. Put them in a saucepan with enough water to cover them. Bring the water to a boil, and boil for 10 minutes. Drain the jars upside down on a clean cloth or rack.

2 If your preserve has not reached setting point, keep the sterilized jars warm in an oven heated to 250°F (130°C). This will prevent the jars from cracking when the hot preserve is spooned into them.

WORKING WITH PRESERVES

• TO MAKE FRUIT JELLIES, cooked fruit is strained overnight through a jelly bag to extract the juice from the pulp. If you do not have a jelly bag, make one by tying the corners of a double thickness of cotton cheesecloth (muslin) over the ingredients to make a bag.

• TO TEST WHETHER JAMS and jellies have reached setting point without using a candy thermometer, spoon a little of the preserve into a saucer and let it cool. Push a finger across the surface. If the surface of the preserve wrinkles, it is ready.

• TO COVER SWEET PRESERVES and chutneys, place a waxed-paper disk over the top, with the waxed side down. The heat of the preserve will melt the wax and protect the top.

• ALWAYS FILL THE JARS while the preserve is still hot. Place cellophane covers on the jars when they are still warm (above left). When the preserve cools, it forms a vacuum, stretching the cellophane cover over the opening (above right).

• VINEGAR-BASED PRESERVES such as pickles, relish, and chutney must be covered with vinegar-proof lids. Glass or cork lids are ideal, or you can use sterilized metal caps if they are lined with waxed paper.

• TO STORE all home-preserved food at room temperature, they must be processed in a hot water bath. Pour on enough hot water to cover the jars by at least 2 inches (5cm) and boil for 15 minutes.

FRUIT VINEGARS

THESE SWEET-AND-SOUR BERRY VINEGARS will enhance many of your friends' favorite dishes.
Presented in their own stamped tote bag, they are the perfect summer gift.

GIFT NEEDS

1¼ cups (300ml) white wine vinegar

1¼ cups (300ml) red wine vinegar

2 jars with lids

1½ cups (270g) fresh or frozen raspberries

1½ cups (270g) fresh or frozen blackberries

2 cups (450g) granulated sugar

Two 10-ounce (300-ml) or four 5-ounce (150-ml) bottles

Makes about 10 ounces (300ml) of each flavored vinegar

PACKAGING NEEDS

Ruler, all-purpose glue, scissors, pencil, tracing paper, felt-tip pen, paper towel, hole punch, tape

Piece of medium-weight craft paper 12 by 18½ inches (30 by 47cm)

Rectangular box or a book to use as a model, 9¼ x 6 x 3 inches (23.5 x 15 x 7.5cm)

Berry stencil (page 59)

Craft foam or close-textured synthetic sponge 2½ by 2½ inches (6.5 by 6.5cm)

Block of wood 2½ by 2½ inches (6.5 by 6.5cm)

Purple acrylic water-based paint

Saucer, to use as a palette

Small craft roller (optional)

24 inches (60cm) shiny cord, for handles

Piece of thick cardboard, 3 by 6 inches (7.5 by 15cm) (optional)

Scraps of craft paper, for gift tags

24 inches (60cm) satin ribbon, ⅛ inch (3mm) wide

Tissue paper, for lining the bag

GIFT: Fruit vinegars

You need to start making the raspberry and blackberry vinegars 12 days in advance.

1 Pour the white wine vinegar into one of the jars and the red wine vinegar into another. Measure out 3 ounces (90g) of each fruit.

2 Add the raspberries to the white wine vinegar and the blackberries to the red wine vinegar and stir well. Screw the lids on the jars and leave in a cool place for 4 days.

3 After 4 days, strain the white wine vinegar into a bowl. Be careful not to press the fruit through the strainer or the vinegar will be cloudy. Return the vinegar to the jar. Repeat with the red wine vinegar.

4 Stir another 3 ounces (90g) of raspberries into the white wine vinegar and 3 ounces (90g) of blackberries into the red wine vinegar. Replace the lids on the jars and leave for 4 more days. Repeat the straining process again, add the remainder of the fruit, and leave for another 4 days. ▶

5 Strain the raspberry vinegar into a saucepan. Add half the sugar and stir over low heat until it dissolves. Boil the vinegar for 5 minutes, skimming the scum off the top, and leave it to cool. Repeat with the blackberry vinegar.

6 Let the vinegars cool and pour into separate bottles. Seal the bottles with corks or other vinegar-proof lids. ▪

GIFTWRAP: Bright berry colors

A homemade tote bag is decorated with a berry shape, stamped on in rich fruity-purple paint.

1 Place the craft paper right side down on a work surface. Using a ruler, measure and turn over ½ inch (1.5cm) on one long side. Glue in place.

2 Place the box lengthwise along the glued edge of the paper. Wrap the paper around the box and glue the overlap in the center.

3 Fold under the excess paper at the bottom of the box, as you would when wrapping a present and glue the overlaps. Leave the box in place to give the bag stability while the glue dries.

4 To make the berry-shaped stamp, trace the pattern on page 59 on tracing paper and cut out the shape with scissors. Place the shape on the square of foam, draw around the outline with a felt-tip pen and cut it out. Glue the foam to the block of wood.

5 Pour a little paint into the saucer, coat the roller, and roll the paint onto the stamp. If you are not using a roller, dip the stamp into the paint and wipe off any excess with a paper towel. Stamp the berry shape randomly over the bag, re-coating the stamp each time. Leave the paint to dry.

6 Carefully remove the box from the bag. Using the hole punch, make two holes on each side of the bag, close to the top and about 1½ inches (4cm) in from each edge.

7 To make the handles, cut the cord in half and bind the ends with tape to prevent fraying. From the inside, thread the two ends of one length of cord through the holes on one side of the bag.

8 Knot the ends of the cord on the outside of the bag, peel off the tape, and trim the ends. Make the other handle the same way. If you wish, cut a piece of cardboard to fit into the bottom of the bag to strengthen it.

9 To make the labels, cut two berry shapes from the scraps of craft paper and punch a hole in the top. Write "Raspberry vinegar" on one and "Blackberry vinegar" on the other with a felt-tip pen. Cut the ribbon in half and tie the labels to the bottles. Line the bag with tissue paper and place the bottles inside. 🎁

Note

Include a card for the recipient with ideas for using the fruit vinegars. Use either vinegar sparingly in salad dressing and in syrup for fruit salad. Add a little to sauces and casseroles, or add a few drops to stir-fried dishes. Take one teaspoon (5ml) of vinegar with hot water or sparkling water as a tonic.

A Trio of Fruit Coulis

THREE FRUIT SAUCES, made from currants and berries,
are packed together in a basket as bright as the fruits themselves.

GIFT NEEDS

Kettle or deep saucepan, blender, funnel (optional), tongs

FOR THE RASPBERRY COULIS

10 ounces (300g) fresh raspberries

1 cup (125g) powdered sugar

About 1 teaspoon (5ml) lemon juice, or to taste

FOR THE BLACKBERRY COULIS

10 ounces (300g) fresh blackberries

1 cup (125g) powdered sugar

About 2 teaspoons (10ml) orange juice, or to taste

FOR THE STRAWBERRY AND
RED CURRANT COULIS

6 ounces (175g) fresh strawberries, hulled

4 ounces (125g) red currants, stalks removed

1 cup (90g) powdered sugar

About 1 tablespoon (15ml) lemon juice, or to taste

Three ½-pint (300-ml) glass jars with screw-on lids

PACKAGING NEEDS

Scissors, iron, needle and thread, hole punch, felt-tip pen, rubber bands

Purple and red acrylic water-based paints

2 small foil containers, to use as palettes

Small paintbrush

Slatted basket with handle; the one used here is 7 x 10 x 4½ inches (18 x 25 x 11.5cm)

Piece of silk 12 by 12 inches (30 by 30cm)

Piece of thick paper 4 by 7 inches (10 by 18cm), for labels

1½ yards (1.5m) satin ribbon, ⅛ inch (3mm) wide

Tissue paper, for packing

GIFT: A trio of fruit coulis

1 Wash the jars and lids, rinse them well, and put them in a kettle or deep saucepan. Cover them with water, bring to a boil, and boil for 10 minutes. Leave the jars in the hot water while you make the sauces.

2 To make the raspberry coulis, put the raspberries and powdered sugar in a blender and process to a puree. Remove one of the jars from the water and stand it upside-down on a clean cloth to drain.

3 Pour the puree into a strainer placed over a bowl. Push the pulp through the strainer with the back of a spoon. Stir in the lemon juice and, if you wish, add a little more to taste.

4 Pour the raspberry coulis into the jar, through a funnel if necessary, to within ½ inch (1.5cm) of the top. Put on the lid and set aside. ▶

5 To make the blackberry coulis, puree the blackberries and powdered sugar in a blender. Place a jar upside-down on a cloth to drain. Strain the pulp as before and stir in the orange juice to taste.

8 Place the jars in the kettle so that they are not touching each other, then pour on more hot water to come to about 2 inches (5cm) above the jars. Bring the water to a boil, cover the kettle, and keep it just boiling for 15 minutes.

6 To make the strawberry and red currant coulis, cut the strawberries in half, discarding any that are discolored. Puree them with the red currants and powdered sugar. Leave a jar to drain while you strain the fruit and stir in the lemon juice to taste.

9 Use tongs to remove the jars from the water and stand them on a wooden rack or a folded cloth. Dry the jars and put them in the refrigerator until you are ready to pack them.

7 Make sure the caps of the three jars are screwed on tightly. Place a folded dish towel or wooden board in a kettle or deep saucepan to keep the bottom of the jars from touching the pan. Half-fill the pan with hot water.

Note

Keep the coulis in the refrigerator for up to one month. However, once the jars have been opened, use the coulis within 10 days.

GIFTWRAP: Color coordinates

Pieces of multicolored checked silk cover the bright jars, which are packed in a basket painted in coordinating berry colors.

1 Pour the paints into the two foil containers. Paint the handle, rim, and alternate slats of the basket purple. Let the paint dry. Paint the remaining slats red and let dry. Apply a second coat if necessary.

2 To make the jar covers, cut three 6-inch (15-cm) squares of silk. To prevent the silk from fraying, turn ¼ inch (6mm) to the wrong side on all four sides and press with an iron. Turn over another ¼ inch (6mm), press, and sew the hem.

3 Cut or tear the thick paper to make three labels and punch a hole in each one. Write the name of each fruit coulis on a label, and write the storage instructions (see Note) on the back with a felt-tip pen.

4 Cut the narrow ribbon into six equal lengths. Cover the jars with the silk squares and secure each with a rubber band and a ribbon. Thread the remaining ribbons through the labels and tie them around the necks of the jars.

5 Pack the basket with crumpled tissue paper and arrange the jars inside, carefully distributing their weight evenly. 🎁

Note

You might like to include storage instructions and serving suggestions written on a note with your gift. Serve over ice cream or with cheesecake.

ROSE-PETAL JELLY

MADE FROM A SIMPLE APPLE JELLY RECIPE, this delicately scented pale pink jelly makes an unusual culinary treat. Wrapped in vibrant colors, this gift is sure to cause a stir.

GIFT NEEDS

1 cup scented rose petals (plus one additional cup of rose petals, optional, see Step 1)

2 cups (500g) granulated sugar

1¾ pounds (875g) cooking apples

3-inch (7.5-cm) strip of lemon zest with all pith removed

2½ cups (600ml) water

Piece of cheesecloth (muslin) 28 by 28 inches (70 by 70cm), or a jelly bag

Two 12-ounce (375-g) decorative glasses or jars

2 waxed-paper disks

2 cellophane preserve jar covers

Makes enough to fill two 12-ounce (375-g) glasses or jars

PACKAGING NEEDS

Pencil, drawing compass or small plate to use as a guide, scissors, pinking shears (optional), hole punch, felt-tip pen, rubber bands

Piece of pink craft paper 15 by 17½ inches (38 by 44.5cm)

Piece of green craft paper or cardboard 4 by 5 inches (10 by 12.5cm), for gift tags

1¾ yards (1.6m) satin ribbon, ⅛ inch (3mm) wide

2 sheets tissue paper in coordinated colors

48 inches (1.2m) wire-edged ribbon, 1 inch (2.5cm) wide

GIFT: Rose-petal jelly

Cook and strain the fruit the day before making the jelly, steps 2 to 4.

1 To increase the rose flavor of the jelly, use rose sugar in place of all or some of the sugar in the recipe. To make rose sugar, put one cup of scented rose petals into a jar, pour on about 2 cups (500g) of sugar, and cover the jar. Shake the jar every few days for at least 1 week. Discard the petals before using.

3 Bring to a boil, then simmer for about 20 minutes or until the fruit is soft. Gently press the fruit against the side of the saucepan once or twice to break it down and release the pectin.

2 Wash the apples and discard any parts that are damaged. Roughly chop the apples, without peeling or coring, and put them in a saucepan with the lemon zest, rose petals, and water.

4 Scald the cheesecloth in boiling water, wring it out, and place it over a bowl. Spoon in the apple pulp. Tie the corners of the cheesecloth together and suspend it over the bowl and leave overnight. Do not squeeze the bag or the jelly will be cloudy. ▶

5 The next day, heat the oven to 250°F (130°C). Meanwhile, discard the contents of the cheesecloth. Measure the juice in the bowl and weigh out the sugar. Allow 2 cups (500g) sugar for every 2½ cups (600ml) juice.

6 Place the sugar on a baking sheet and warm it in the oven for 15 minutes. Wash and sterilize the glass containers following the instructions on page 54.

7 Pour the fruit juice into a saucepan and add the warmed sugar. Stir over low heat until the sugar has dissolved. Increase the heat and bring to a boil. Boil rapidly for 10 to 15 minutes, skimming off scum as it rises.

Note

You can also make rosemary jelly following the same basic recipe. Substitute three or four sprigs of fresh rosemary for the rose petals when cooking the apples. At Step 9, when the jelly has reached setting point, stir in 1 tablespoon (15ml) of white wine vinegar. Pour the jelly into the warmed glasses or jars and push a sprig of rosemary into each one.

8 Test the jelly for set by spooning a little onto a cold saucer. When it is cool, push a finger across the surface. The surface will wrinkle when the jelly is ready.

9 When the setting point is reached, pour the jelly into the glasses. Cover with waxed disks and secure a cellophane cover over each glass with a rubber band. Store in the refrigerator and use within one month. ▪▪

GIFTWRAP: Jelly surprise

Glasses of pink jelly are wrapped in layers of vibrant lime and forest green tissue paper to create a fun and modern look.

1 Using a pencil and compass or a small plate, draw and cut out of the craft paper two circles 4 inches (10cm) larger in diameter than the glasses. Scallop the edges or use pinking shears for an interesting finish.

2 To make the gift tags, draw two leaf shapes on the green paper. Cut them out with scissors and punch a hole in the top of each one before writing your message.

3 Remove the cellophane covers from the glasses and put on the pink paper covers, secured with rubber bands. Cut two 24-inch (60-cm) lengths of the narrow ribbon. Wind the ribbon twice around each glass, tie a bow, and trim the ends with scissors.

4 Cut the two sheets of tissue paper and the wide ribbon in half. Put two halves of different colored paper on top of each other and place one of the glasses in the center. Pull up the corners of the paper over the glass and tie the ribbon around it in a bow.

5 Wrap the other glass in the same way. Cut the remaining narrow ribbon in half. Thread the lengths of ribbon through the holes in the gift tags and tie them to the wide ribbon, next to the bow. ▓

Note

You can also present the rose-petal jelly in a simple basket lined with gingham napkins. Tie matching jar covers on with raffia.

CORN AND PEPPER RELISH

THIS SPICY, BRIGHT YELLOW RELISH, presented in an aromatic herb basket,
is a feast for all the senses – perfect for barbecues and picnics.

GIFT NEEDS

Kettle or deep saucepan, tongs

3 large ears of corn or 10 ounces (300g) frozen corn kernels

4 ounces (125g) yellow pepper

4 ounces (125g) green pepper

6 ounces (175g) red pepper

2 red chilies

4 ounces (125g) celery

4 ounces (125g) onion

½ cup (120ml) cider vinegar

½ cup (120ml) water

1 tablespoon salt

1 teaspoon dry mustard

2 tablespoons sugar

2 teaspoons mustard seed

2 teaspoons onion seed or onion powder

1 teaspoon black pepper

Three 9-ounce (275-ml) preserving jars with vinegar-proof lids

Makes about 27 ounces (825ml) of relish

PACKAGING NEEDS

All-purpose glue, scissors, hole punch, ink pen

Basket with slatted sides, about 6 by 8 inches (15 by 20cm)

About 40 stems of fresh thyme or rosemary

3 dried chilies, for decoration

Spray-on varnish or clear water-based varnish and small paintbrush

Piece of medium-weight cardboard

12 inches (30cm) satin ribbon, ⅛ inch (3mm) wide

Dried corn husks, or tissue paper and some fresh or dried bay leaves

GIFT: Corn and pepper relish

Make the relish about one week in advance. Warm the preserving jars in the oven at 250°F (130°C) and soak the rubber rings in hot water.

1 If using corn on the cob, carefully strip off the kernels with a sharp knife. Put the fresh or frozen corn kernels into a large saucepan.

2 Halve the yellow, green, and red peppers and discard the center core and seeds. Chop the peppers finely and add them to the corn.

3 Prepare the chilies in the same way, discarding the seeds and chopping the flesh finely. Add the chilies to the saucepan. Remember to wash your hands after touching chilies or use rubber gloves if your skin is sensitive.

4 Chop the celery and onion finely and add it to the saucepan. Stir all the vegetables to mix them thoroughly. ▶

5 In a small bowl, mix together the vinegar, water, salt, and dry mustard. Pour the mixture over the vegetables and stir well.

6 Add the sugar, mustard seed, onion seed, and black pepper to the saucepan. Stir well and bring the mixture to a boil.

7 Cook over medium heat, stirring frequently, for 15 minutes, or until the vegetables are just tender. Add a little more vinegar and water if the mixture becomes too dry. Taste, and adjust the seasoning if necessary. Spoon the relish into the warmed jars.

8 Remove the rubber rings from the water, dry them, and put them on the lids. Place the closed jars on a wooden board or a folded dish towel in a kettle or deep saucepan half-filled with hot water.

9 Pour on more hot water so that the jars are covered by about 2 inches (5cm) of water. Bring to a boil, cover the saucepan and process the jars (see page 55), with the water still boiling, for 15 minutes.

10 Lift the jars out of the saucepan with tongs. Stand the jars on a board or folded cloth and leave them to cool. ▪▪

GIFTWRAP: Aromatic basket

*The jars of relish are decorated with varnished chilies, and packed together
with dried corn husks in a slatted basket woven with fresh herbs.*

1 Starting at the bottom of the
basket and working around it,
weave the herb stems in and out of the
slats, joining in more stems as you go.

2 Continue weaving the stems
until the sides of the basket are
covered. Tuck in any unsightly stem
ends behind the tips of others.

3 Spray or paint the chilies with
two coats of varnish, letting each
coat dry between applications. Glue a
chili to the top of each jar.

4 To make labels, cut out three
rectangles from the cardboard.
Make a hole in the labels with a hole
punch before writing your message.

5 Cut the ribbon in thirds and tie
the labels to the jars. Line the
basket with dried corn husks, or with
tissue paper and a few bay leaves,
before adding the jars of relish. 🎁

Note

*The flavor of the relish improves
with age, so make the relish about
one week in advance. Include a note
to store the relish in a refrigerator
and use within one month.*

ORANGE AND APPLE MARMALADE

THIS TANGY PRESERVE, lightly spiced with coriander seeds, adds an exotic touch
to any breakfast table. The sunny packaging is sure to get the day off to a bright start.

GIFT NEEDS

Kettle or deep saucepan, baking sheet, tongs, drawing compass or small plate to use as a guide, pencil, pinking shears (optional), tape, rubber bands, safety matches, white household candle

1 pound (500g) oranges

1 pound (500g) cooking apples

2 teaspoons coriander seeds, lightly crushed

Piece of cotton cheesecloth (muslin) 8 by 8 inches (20 by 20cm)

2 cups (450ml) water

Three 8-ounce (250-g) preserve jars or terra-cotta pots with cork lids

2 cups (500g) granulated sugar

3 waxed-paper disks

3 pieces of silk or cotton 7 by 7 inches (18 by 18cm)

¾ yard (75cm) colored raffia

Makes enough to fill three 8-ounce (225-g) jars

PACKAGING NEEDS

Scissors, all-purpose glue, pencil, tape, double-sided tape

FOR EACH JAR OF MARMALADE

Canister or tin large enough to hold the jar, about 4¼ inches (11cm) in diameter and 4½ inches (11.5cm) deep

Sheet of wrapping paper with fruit design

Sheet of plain or striped paper to use as border

Piece of medium-weight cardboard, at least 4½ by 4½ inches (11.5 by 11.5cm)

Strip of thinner cardboard, 1 inch (2.5cm) wide and the length of the circumference of the lid

Tissue paper, for packing

GIFT: Orange and apple marmalade

1 Wash the oranges and cut them into segments, but do not peel them. Cut away and discard the white fiber and reserve the seeds. Roughly cut the segments according to whether you prefer a fine or chunky preserve.

2 Wash the apples. Peel and core them but reserve the peel and cores. Roughly chop the apples into 1-inch (2.5-cm) cubes.

3 Put the orange seeds, apple peel and cores, and the crushed coriander seeds into the center of the cheesecloth. Tie the opposite corners together to make a bag.

4 Put the oranges, apples, and the spice bag into a kettle or deep saucepan, and pour in the water. Bring slowly to a boil and simmer until the orange peel is tender, about 1 hour. ▶

5 Put the cork lids in a saucepan of water and bring it to a boil. Meanwhile, spread the sugar on a baking sheet and warm it in the oven set at 250°F (130°C) for 15 minutes. Warm the jars in the oven at the same time.

6 Remove the sugar from the oven and stir it into the fruit over a low heat, until the sugar has dissolved. Lift out the spice bag with tongs, squeeze it to extract all the fruit juice, and discard.

7 Turn up the heat and bring to a boil, or until the preserve reaches 250°F (130°C) on a candy thermometer. Boil, stirring frequently, until the preserve sets, about 10 minutes.

8 To test that the marmalade has reached setting point, spoon a little onto a cold saucer. Let it cool, then push a finger across the top. When it is ready, the surface should wrinkle.

9 Pour the preserve into the jars and put a waxed disk on top. Drain the cork lids and put them on the jars. To seal the jars, light the candle and melt the wax to seal around the lid. Store in the refrigerator and use within one month.

10 To make the jar covers, use a pencil and compass or a small plate to draw three circles on the silk, about 3 inches (7.5cm) larger in diameter than the jars. To prevent fraying, cut out the circles with pinking shears or put strips of tape over the outlines first. Fit the silk over the jars, secure with a rubber band and raffia. ▪▪

GIFTWRAP: A fruitful image

*For each gift, a canister is decorated with a decoupage of fruit shapes,
hinting at its fruity contents.*

1 To cover each canister, cut out a variety of fruit shapes from the wrapping paper and glue them around the side so that they overlap each other.

2 From the border paper, cut two strips 1 inch (2.5cm) wide and as long as the circumference of the canister. Glue the strips around the top and bottom of the canister to cover the edges of the fruit shapes.

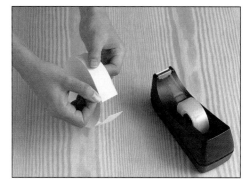

3 To make each lid, use the canister as a guide to draw a circle on the medium-weight cardboard. Draw a circle $1/8$ inch (3mm) larger than the canister and cut it out with scissors. Attach the thinner cardboard strip to the circle with strips of tape.

4 Cut a piece of border paper 2 inches (5cm) wide and as long as the circumference of the lid. Cover the back with double-sided tape and peel off the backing paper. Position the lid on its side in the center of the paper and smooth the paper around the lid.

5 Use scissors to snip the overlap at $1/4$-inch (6-mm) intervals and fold the paper over the top and inside the rim. Cut a circle of wrapping paper to fit the top of the lid, cover it with double-sided tape, and press it onto the lid.

6 Line each canister with tissue paper before putting the jars of orange and apple marmalade inside. ▓

APRICOT SPREAD

ENLIVEN YOUR BREAKFAST TOAST OR AFTER-SCHOOL SANDWICH with this delicate fruit spread, enriched with butter, eggs, and sugar and presented in a decorative stucco box.

GIFT NEEDS

Heatproof bowl to fit over a saucepan or a double boiler, whisk, rubber bands, pencil, drawing compass or small dish to use as a guide, scissors

12 ounces (375g) fresh apricots

1½ cups (375g) granulated sugar

½ cup (100ml) water

3 eggs, plus 3 egg whites

½ cup (1 stick) unsalted butter, cut into pieces

3 tablespoons (45ml) lemon juice

1 teaspoon grated lemon zest

Two 12-ounce (375-g) decorative glasses or jars

2 waxed-paper disks

2 cellophane preserve jar covers

Piece of cotton cheesecloth (muslin), 7 by 12 inches (18 by 30cm)

Piece of cotton netting (gauze), 7 by 12 inches (18 by 30cm)

48 inches (1.2m) satin ribbon, ⅛ inch (3mm) wide

Makes about 24 ounces (750g)

PACKAGING NEEDS

Palette knife or spreader, scissors, felt-tip pen, all-purpose glue

Blue and pale orange water-based latex paints

2 small foil containers, to use as palettes

Small paintbrush

Wooden, cardboard, or papier-mâché box, about 7½ inches (19cm) in diameter and 4 inches (10cm) deep, to fit the two glasses

2 large foil containers and 2 sticks, for mixing the plaster

About 4 ounces (125g) plaster of Paris

Piece of cardboard 2 by 2 inches (5 by 5cm), for gift tag

Tissue paper, for packing

¾ yard (70cm) each of two sheer ribbons, 1¼ inches (4.5cm) wide

GIFT: Apricot spread

Sterilize two 12-ounce (375-g) decorative glasses or jars following the instructions on page 54.

1 Wash the apricots and cut them into quarters. Put the apricots and stones in a saucepan with ½ cup (125g) of the sugar and the water. Cook over low heat, stirring occasionally, for about 15 minutes or until the fruit is soft.

2 Place a strainer over a bowl, pour in the fruit mixture, and press it through the strainer with the back of a spoon. Remove the stones and continue to press out as much fruit pulp as possible.

3 Pour about 2 inches (5cm) of water into a saucepan and heat until simmering. Put the fruit puree into a heatproof bowl that fits over the saucepan without touching the water. Alternatively, use a double boiler.

4 Place the saucepan and bowl over a very low heat. Meanwhile, lightly whisk the eggs and egg whites together until the mixture is foamy. ▶

5 Add the egg mixture, the remaining sugar, and the butter to the fruit puree. Stir or whisk over the simmering water for about 40 minutes or until the mixture has the consistency of thick honey.

6 Carefully remove the bowl from the saucepan and place on a work surface. Stir in the lemon juice and lemon zest.

7 While the apricot spread is still hot, pour it into the two sterilized glasses. Place waxed-paper disks on the apricot spread and cover the glasses with cellophane. Hold the cellophane in place with a rubber band.

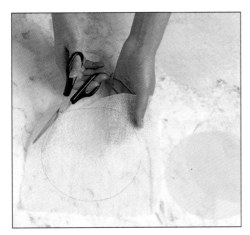

Note

You can also make a tangy plum spread in the same way. Simply substitute 12 ounces (375g) fresh plums for the apricots in the recipe.

8 To make the cloth covers, draw two circles about 6 inches (15cm) in diameter on the cheesecloth and netting, using the compass or a small plate, and a pencil. Cut out the circles.

9 Cover each glass with a circle of cheesecloth and then with a circle of the netting. Cut the ribbon in half and tie on the covers, winding the ribbon around the glasses twice before tying a bow. Store in the refrigerator. ▪

GIFTWRAP: Stucco paint

The gift box, decorated with a paint and plaster mixture that creates the texture of frosting, will be admired long after the apricot spread is finished.

1 Pour a little of each paint into foil containers. Paint the inside and the base of the box pale orange and leave it upside down to dry. Paint the inside of the lid blue and let it dry.

2 Pour some pale orange paint into a large foil container and stir in enough plaster powder to make a thick, spreading consistency. Stir in a little water if the mixture becomes too thick.

3 Using the palette knife, swirl the plaster mixture around the side of the box. Spread the mixture on thinly at the top, so that the lid will still fit. Mix up more paint and plaster if necessary. Let the box dry.

4 Mix some blue paint with plaster powder as described in Step 2, and spread it over the top and sides of the lid. Let it dry.

5 Cut out a gift tag from the piece of cardboard. Write a message to tell the recipient that the apricot spread will keep in the refrigerator for up to three weeks.

6 Line the box with tissue paper before adding the gift and gift tag. To decorate the lid, tie the sheer ribbons into a bow, then tie a second bow with the ends of the first. Trim the ends and glue the bow to the lid. 🎁

Apple Squares

Made with only fresh fruit and sugar, this apple preserve sets to the consistency of gumdrops and, like that confection, is sure to please.

GIFT NEEDS

Deep saucepan, baking sheet

2½ pounds (1.25kg) cooking apples

2 cups (500ml) water

Pared zest of 1 lemon

3 cups (750g) granulated sugar

8-inch (20-cm) square pan

Powdered sugar, for dusting

Makes about 1½ pounds (750g)

PACKAGING NEEDS

Ruler, pencil, felt-tip pen, craft knife, cutting mat, double-sided tape, tracing paper, masking tape, paper towel, all-purpose glue, scissors, parchment paper

Piece of medium-weight cardboard 10½ by 10½ inches (26 by 26cm)

Piece of acetate 9½ by 9½ inches (25 by 25cm)

Scrap of cardboard, about 3 by 3 inches (7.5 by 7.5cm), to use for the stencil

Apple stencil (page 82)

Green and red acrylic water-based or ceramic paints

Gold craft paint

4 small foil containers, to use as palettes

2 small stencil brushes

48 inches (1.2m) printed sheer ribbon, 1½ inches (4cm) wide

GIFT: Apple squares

Preheat the oven to 250°F (130°C) and brush an 8-inch (20-cm) square pan with oil.

1 Wash and roughly chop the apples. Put them in a heavy-based saucepan with the water and lemon zest. Bring to a boil and simmer for about 20 minutes, until the fruit is soft.

2 Pass the fruit through a vegetable mill or press though a coarse strainer over a bowl. Return the puree to the rinsed saucepan and cook over a low heat, stirring frequently, until it is dry and forms a paste, about 40 minutes.

3 Meanwhile, spread the sugar on a baking sheet and warm it in the preheated oven for about 20 minutes. Spoon the warmed sugar into the saucepan and stir until it dissolves.

4 Continue cooking, stirring frequently, until the paste is gingery brown in color. It may take up to 1½ hours to reach this stage. ▶

5 Spoon the paste into the prepared pan and spread it out evenly. Let it cool and refrigerate. When the paste has set after about 2 hours, cut it into squares with a knife dipped in hot water. Toss the squares in powdered sugar and set aside until you are ready to package them. ▪▪

GIFTWRAP: Stenciled box

The gilded-apple stencil on the transparent box denotes the flavor of the candy it contains.

1 To make the box base, measure and draw lines 1¼ inches (3cm) in from each edge of the cardboard. Score along the lines with a craft knife and cut right through one of the lines at each corner section, to form the overlaps.

2 Place a piece of double-sided tape at each corner. Turn the cardboard over and fold along the scored lines. Remove the backing paper from the tape and press the corners together.

3 To make the lid, use a felt-tip pen and ruler to measure and lightly mark lines ½ inch (2cm) in from each edge of the acetate. Cut along one edge of each corner section but do not fold the corners yet.

4 To make the apple stencil, trace the outline of the apple on this page on tracing paper, then transfer the design to the scrap of cardboard. Cut out the outline with a craft knife.

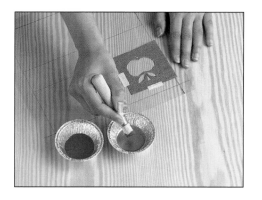

5 Measure and lightly mark a strip 1½ inches (4cm) wide across the center of the lid. This is where the ribbon will be attached and needs to be kept free of decoration.

6 Pour a little green and gold paint into separate foil containers. Anchor the apple stencil in place with masking tape. Dip one brush first into the green paint and then into the gold. Dab off any excess on paper towel and stencil the stem and leaves. Let it dry.

7 Pour a little red and gold paint into separate foil containers. Dip the other stencil brush first into the red paint and then into the gold. Dab off any excess paint on a paper towel and stencil the fruit. Reposition the stencil, and repeat the pattern across the lid.

8 When the paint has dried, cut an 11-inch (27½-cm) length of ribbon and cover it with double-sided tape. Peel off the backing paper and press the ribbon across the center of the lid with about ½ inch (2cm) extending over the edge of the acetate. Turn the overlap over and press it to the inside of the lid.

9 To complete the lid, use a ruler to help fold the sides along the marked lines and then fold in and glue the corner flaps where they overlap.

10 Line the box with parchment paper before adding the apple squares. Shape the remaining ribbon into a bow and trim the ends. Attach the bow to the ribbon band with double-sided tape. ❖

BLUEBERRY MOLD

THIS FIRM, FRESH-FRUIT PRESERVE is set in two decorative molds. Turn it out and serve it as the perfect accompaniment to cold meats, poultry, and game.

GIFT NEEDS

Deep saucepan, baking sheet

1¼ pounds (625g) blueberries

1 cup (250g) granulated sugar

2 tablespoons (30ml) lemon juice

Two-4-ounce (150-ml) molds or containers

2 waxed-paper disks

2 cellophane preserve jar covers

2 rubber bands

Fills two 4-ounce (150-ml) molds or containers

PACKAGING NEEDS

Pencil, compass or small plate to use as a guide, scissors, rubber bands, ruler, all-purpose glue, hole punch, tape, felt-tip pen

Piece of striped paper, 12 by 14 inches (30 by 35cm)

24 inches (60cm) narrow cord

Piece of purple craft paper, 8 by 21 inches (20 by 53.5cm)

Rectangular box to use as model, the one used here is 7 x 4½ x 3 inches (18 x 11.5 x 7.5cm)

24 inches (60cm) medium cord

Piece of thin cardboard 2¼ by 4½ inches (6 by 12cm), for gift tag

Piece of thick cardboard 3 by 7 inches (7.5 by 18cm)

Tissue paper, for packing

4 inches (10cm) satin ribbon, ⅛ inch (3mm) wide

GIFT: Blueberry mold

Preheat the oven to 250°F (130°C) and lightly brush two ¼-pint (150-ml) molds with vegetable oil.

1 Wash the blueberries and discard any stalks. Put them in a saucepan and simmer for about 15 minutes, or until the blueberries are soft.

2 Place a strainer over a bowl and pour in the blueberries. Press the fruit through the strainer with the back of a spoon, extracting as much of the fruit pulp as possible.

3 Rinse the saucepan and pour the fruit puree in. Cook over a low heat until the puree thickens and there is no visible liquid, about 20 minutes. Spread the sugar on a baking sheet and warm it in the preheated oven for 15 minutes.

4 Put the warmed sugar into the saucepan and stir until it has dissolved. Turn up the heat a little and cook, stirring constantly, until the spoon leaves a wide trail in the puree. ▶

5 Stir in the lemon juice and remove the pan from the heat. Let the puree cool slightly before spooning it into the greased molds. Place a waxed-paper disk on top of each blueberry mold to seal it. Then cover the top of each container with a cellophane cover, and secure it with a rubber band. Keep the molds refrigerated until you are ready to pack them. ▪▪

Note

For a welcome gift at Thanksgiving, make cranberry molds in the same way. Use 3 cups (700g) cranberries and add ½ cup (125ml) water in Step 3 and 2½ cups (500 g) sugar in step 4.

GIFTWRAP: Blueberry-colored tote

The glass molds are topped with candy-striped paper, which coordinates with the gift tag on the bag.

1 Using a pencil and compass or small plate, draw circles with a diameter about 3 inches (7.5cm) larger than the molds onto the striped paper . Cut out the circles with scissors.

2 Remove the cellophane cover from each mold and replace with a paper circle; secure with a rubber band. Cut the narrow cord in half and knot all the ends to prevent fraying. Tie the cord around the molds in a knot.

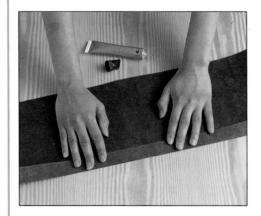

3 To make the tote bag, place the craft paper right side down on the work surface. Fold over a 1-inch (2.5-cm) strip along one of the long sides and glue it down.

4 Put the box on the paper, with one long edge level with the folded edge. Wrap the paper around the box and glue the overlap down the center.

5 Fold over the excess paper at the bottom of the box, as you would when wrapping a present, and glue it in place. Leave the box inside the bag while the glue dries, then remove it.

6 Using the hole punch, make two holes on each side of the bag, close to the top and about 1³⁄₄ inches (4.5cm) in from each side.

7 Cut the medium cord in half and bind the ends with tape to prevent fraying. From the outside, thread the two ends of a length of cord through the punched holes on one side of the bag.

8 Knot the ends, peel off the tape, and trim off any excess. Make the other handle in the same way. Cover one side of the small piece of cardboard with striped paper and write the storage instructions (see Note) inside.

9 Place the piece of thick cardboard in the base of the bag to strengthen it. Stand the glass molds in the bag and pack crumpled tissue paper around them. Use the hole punch to make a hole in the gift tag and tie it to the handle with the ribbon. 🎁

Note

Write the following storage details and serving suggestions on the gift tag tied to the tote bag.
Store the blueberry mold in the refrigerator for up to one month. Serve it with sliced cold meat, poultry, or game.

CHOW-CHOW RELISH

THIS POPULAR MUSTARD RELISH, presented in a colorful string container,
is perfect with homemade burgers and open-face cheese sandwiches.

GIFT NEEDS

Kettle or deep saucepan, slotted spoon

4 ounces (125g) small cucumbers (gherkins)

4 ounces (125g) red pepper

4 ounces (125g) green pepper

3 ounces (90g) small green beans

4 ounces (125g) cauliflower

2 ounces (60g) small young carrots

2 ounces (60g) small onions

1 cup (250g) coarse salt

Two 12-ounce (375-g) preserving jars with cork lids

2 cups (450ml) cider vinegar

4 teaspoons all-purpose flour

1 tablespoon dry mustard

1 teaspoon ground turmeric

2 teaspoons granulated sugar

1 teaspoon celery seed

2 waxed-paper disks

White household candle and matches

Fills two 12-ounce (375-g) preserving jars

PACKAGING NEEDS

All-purpose glue, pencil, scissors, cutting mat, craft knife, tape, double-sided tape

Oval or round cardboard, papier-mâché, or plastic food container large enough to hold the 2 jars, the one used here is 7½ x 3½ x 6 inches (18 x 9 x 15cm)

About 10 feet (3m) each string or cord in three colors (see Note)

Piece of thick cardboard, 5 by 8 inches (13 by 20cm), for the lid

Strip of thinner cardboard, 1-inch (2.5-cm) wide and as long as the circumference of the lid

Piece of corrugated cardboard, 10 by 20 inches (25 by 50cm)

Tissue paper, for packing

GIFT: Chow-chow relish

Make the relish about 2 weeks in advance so it has a chance to mature. Salt the vegetables at least 12 hours before you make the relish.

1 Cut the cucumbers into ⅛-inch (4-mm) slices. Halve the peppers, discard the core and seeds, and cut into ½-inch (1.5-cm) squares. Cut the beans into ½-inch (1.5-cm) lengths and the cauliflower into small flowerets. Peel the carrots and cut them into ⅛-inch (4-mm) slices. Peel and halve the onions.

2 Put the vegetables in a large china or glass bowl (not a metal one), sprinkling some of the salt between each layer. Cover the bowl and let stand for about 12 hours or overnight.

3 Sterilize the jars and cork lids following the instructions given on pages 54–55. Leave the jars and the lids in the water.

4 Spoon the vegetables into a colander in two or three batches. Rinse off the salt thoroughly under cold running water and drain well. ►

5 Put the vinegar into a heatproof enamel, glass, or stainless steel saucepan and add the vegetables. Stir well, bring to a boil, and then simmer for 5 minutes.

6 Remove the saucepan from the heat. Lift out the vegetables with a slotted spoon and put them in a bowl. Keep the vinegar in the saucepan.

7 In a small bowl, mix together the flour, dry mustard, and turmeric. Pour on a little of the hot vinegar and mix to a smooth paste.

8 Add the paste to the vinegar in the saucepan. Add the sugar and celery seed and return to the heat. Bring to a boil, stirring constantly, then simmer for 2 minutes. Turn off the heat, add the vegetables, and coat in the sauce.

9 Remove the cork lids from the water and let drain. Remove the jars, dry them on the outside, and stand them upside down on a clean cloth or board to drain. Spoon the pickle into the jars.

10 Cover the surface of the pickle with a waxed-paper disk, then add the cork lids. Let the jars cool a little, then melt wax around the rim of the jar between the container and the lid. Keep in the refrigerator and use in a month. ▪

GIFTWRAP: String wrapping

Wrap an oval food storage container with bands of different-colored string. Once the relish has been enjoyed, the box will be a colorful addition to any kitchen .

1 To decorate the container with string, spread a line of glue just below the line where the existing lid overlaps the side. Press the first color of string on the glue.

2 Apply another line of glue below the first and wind the string around the container. Continue gluing and winding, pressing each line of string close to the one before. When you have made a band of color, cut the string and begin with another color. Continue until the box is covered.

3 To make a lid for the container, draw around the top of the box on the thick cardboard and cut out the shape. Cut a strip of the thinner cardboard as long as the circumference of the lid. Use small strips of tape to attach the piece for the side to the piece for the top.

4 To cover the lid, measure and cut out the corrugated cardboard to the same size as the top and the side of the lid. Cover both pieces of corrugated cardboard with double-sided tape. Peel off the backing paper and stick the pieces to the lid.

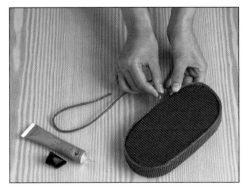

5 Cut a length of string to fit around the rim of the lid. Spread a line of glue where the side and top meet and press on a length of string. ⌘

> ### Note
>
> *If you cannot find string in the colors you want, buy white string and dye it with commercial dye. You can also use food coloring mixed with water and 1 tablespoon (15ml) of vinegar.*

Crafting with Fruit & Vegetables

❦ CREATE A VARIETY OF UNUSUAL gifts for family and friends using fruits, nuts, and vegetables. Present a garland of dried apple and orange slices and bay leaves in a handmade papier-mâché bowl or a rustic heart-shaped wreath of nuts, cones, and dried berries in a forest-green box stamped with gold hearts. Bundles of fresh baby vegetables arranged on a wreath make a bountiful gift, and a set of citrus place markers in a lime-green and blue box will delight the family.

There are seasonal ideas, too. Enter into the spirit of Halloween with a basket of squash candle lamps. Add sparkle at Christmas with decorations made from kumquats, spices, and chilies, a centerpiece of frosted and gilded fruits packed in a gold-leaf box, or a glistening cranberry topiary tree, presented in an elegant pyramid box.

WORKING WITH WREATHS

WREATHS ADORNED WITH FLOWERS, fruits, and vegetables have been symbols of welcome and friendship since the earliest times. A decorated wreath will make an inspired traditional gift.

WREATHS TO MAKE AND BUY You can make your own wreath base from supple twigs that naturally twist and entwine, such as clematis or young grapevine stems. Join them into a circle with more of the same twigs. For wreaths with a less open look, bind a handful of long grass stems or unripened wheat or oat stalks over and over with more of the same, or with raffia, joining in more stalks as needed. You can also buy ready-made twig, stem, straw, and raffia wreath bases or absorbent foam rings. Build up a collection of wreaths and you can decorate them as impromptu gifts throughout the year.

SECURING THE DECORATION The three basic ways of fixing decorative materials to stem wreath bases are gluing, binding, and piercing (see right). The method you use will depend on the type of decoration chosen; the fixing material should always be hidden by the decoration. Foam wreath bases are usually wrapped with binding or pierced.

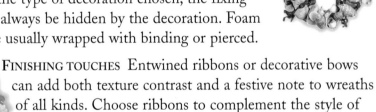

FINISHING TOUCHES Entwined ribbons or decorative bows can add both texture contrast and a festive note to wreaths of all kinds. Choose ribbons to complement the style of your finished wreath. Rustic and countrified designs look great with raffia or hessian bows. Romantic wreath styles are enhanced by sheer ribbon bows or bows tied with several ribbons in coordinated colors. Candles add a further dimension to table wreaths – arrange a cluster of candles around a fresh flower wreath or place a thick candle in the center. Make sure you press plastic candle spikes, available from florists, into the foam ring to secure the candles before you finish the flower arrangement.

WREATH BASICS

- MAKE YOUR OWN wreath base by braiding bundles of straw or raffia. Bend the braid into a circle as you work and secure with straw or raffia.

- ALL KINDS OF MATERIAL can be used to fix decorations to wreaths, from string to wire. Even the material the wreath is made of, such as raffia or straw, can be used to bind objects to a wreath base. Use floral pins or floral wires bent in a U shape to attach tied bundles of items to braided wreaths.

DECORATING WREATHS

- To enhance a natural wreath base simply, try binding a wide ribbon loosely around it. Or you could wrap a foam wreath base in overlapping bands of ribbon to cover it completely (right).

- Heavy decorations, such as large sprays of foliage or pine cones, are usually bound to a wreath so the binding material is concealed. Among the natural options are raffia, twine, sisal, and green garden string.

- Piercing is suitable for securing lightweight foliage sprays, bundles of vegetables or spices, and posies of dried flowers. Stick the wire through the bundle and then into the wreath at a horizontal angle.

- A trip to the beach can provide inspiration for decoration. Use all-purpose glue to fix shells and seaweed to a wreath, or gather nuts and cones, on a nature walk. Alternatively, glue dried fruit and bundles of cinnamon and other spices.

- Foam bases are practical but not decorative, and need to be completely concealed. Take care to angle plants down over both the inner and outer rims of the wreath so that no foam is visible from any angle.

- Add a romantic touch to a table wreath by including candles, anchored in the foam base with plastic spikes. Absorbent foam wreath bases soaked in water provide moisture for fresh flowers. Spray the wreath daily to keep the foam moist.

GARLAND OF DRIED FRUITS

DRIED APPLE AND ORANGE RINGS interspersed with bay leaves make a decorative
garland that can be hung on a wall, perhaps over a picture frame or mirror.

GIFT NEEDS

Sharp kitchen knife, scissors

2 small oranges and 2 small blood oranges or 4 small oranges

3 small cooking apples

2 wire cooling racks

About 20 fresh or dried bay leaves

30 inches (76cm) thin, flexible wire

1½ yards (1.5m) wire-edged checked ribbon, 1½ inches (4cm) wide

Wire cutters

PACKAGING NEEDS

Ruler, paper towel, tall jar or can, craft glue, thin-bladed kitchen knife or palette knife, scissors or craft knife

Scrap paper such as newspaper or used computer paper

Bowl to use as a mold; the one used here is 9 inches (23cm) in diameter and 4 inches (10cm) deep

Petroleum jelly

3 or 4 small foil containers, to use as palettes

Small stick, for stirring

Small paintbrush

Fine-grit sandpaper (optional)

Dark red and dark blue acrylic water-based paints

Gold metallic pen or gold acrylic paint and fine-pointed craft paintbrush

Clear water-based varnish

Tissue paper (optional, see Note)

GIFT: Garland of dried fruits
Preheat the oven to 250°F (130°C)

1 Slice the oranges and apples into rings about ¼ inch (6mm) thick using a sharp knife, and place them on cooling racks. Put them in the preheated oven with the door slightly ajar for three to four hours, or until the fruit feels dry. The exact time will depend on the moisture content of the fruit.

2 When the fruit is cool, divide the orange and apple slices and the bay leaves into two equal groups, so that you can easily make the garland symmetrical. Start by threading a few bay leaves onto the middle of the wire.

3 Working on one half of the garland first, thread on two or three orange slices, then a few apple slices. Or alternate orange and apple slices.

4 Thread on bay leaves at intervals between the slices, to provide color contrast. When half of the slices and leaves have been threaded, compose the second half of the garland to match the first. ▶

5 Cut the ribbon into thirds and trim the ends into a V shape with scissors. Tie a bow on each end of the garland and knot the third ribbon around the center of the garland.

6 Twist the ends of the flexible wire into loops for hanging and trim any excess wire with wire cutters. ▪▪

GIFTWRAP: Molded and painted bowl

After receiving the gift, the recipient will have a decorative, handmade papier-mâché bowl to display such things as fruit or painted eggs.

1 To make the paper scraps for the papier mâché, place several sheets of paper together and press a ruler down firmly about 1½ inches (4cm) from one edge. Tear the paper along the ruler. Cut or tear the strips into squares. The exact size is not critical, but small scraps of paper are easier to mold.

3 Pour some craft glue into a small container and dilute it with a little water to give a thin consistency. Mix the glue and water thoroughly.

2 Rub petroleum jelly liberally over the outside of the bowl with a paper towel. The jelly will make it easier to unmold the finished paper shape when it has dried. When the bowl is thoroughly greased, invert it over a tall jar or can.

4 Put the scraps of paper in cold water and then put them on the surface of the bowl, patchwork style, leaving no gaps. Let this first layer dry for a few minutes, then paste over a small area at a time with glue. Press on more scraps, pasting over each one.

5 Dilute more glue if necessary. Continue adding and pasting more paper scraps until you have 12 to 15 layers or the thickness on the bowl is about ⅛ inch (3mm). The number of layers needed depends on the thickness of paper used. Brush over the final layer (see Note) with more diluted glue.

6 Set the bowl aside, still upside-down on the jar, in a warm, airy place for several days. When the paper bowl is completely dry, insert a knife blade between the bowl and the mold to break the vacuum. Gently twist the bowl and ease the papier mâché away.

7 Trim the rim with sharp scissors or a craft knife to give a smooth edge. If necessary, sand the rim with a small piece of fine-grit sandpaper.

Note

To achieve a rough-textured finish on the bowl, use tissue paper as the final layer. Tear the paper into roughly 3-inch (7.5-cm) squares. Pick up each square on a brush and drop it over the bowl so that it falls in folds and creases.

8 Pour some red paint into a container. Invert the bowl on the jar or can and paint the outside of the bowl. Let it dry. Apply a second coat of paint and let it dry.

9 Paint the inside of the bowl with two coats of blue paint, allowing each one to dry. With the gold metallic pen, draw a fine gold line around the rim, or use gold paint and a fine paintbrush. When the bowl is dry, paint both inside and out with 2 or 3 coats of varnish, letting each coat dry. ✿

HEART-SHAPED HARVEST WREATH

GATHER TOGETHER A SELECTION OF NUTS AND CONES, small fruits, and
leaf sprays to decorate a heart-shaped wreath that will last.

GIFT NEEDS

All-purpose glue

1–2 sprays of eucalyptus leaves

5–6 sprays of dried blueberries or other small berries

About 8 ounces (250g) of nuts in the shell, including almonds, brazils, chestnuts, filberts, and pecans

2–3 litchis

10–12 small pine and larch cones

Heart-shaped wreath form about 9 by 10 inches (23 by 25cm)

PACKAGING NEEDS

Pencil, ruler, craft knife, cutting mat, tracing paper, felt-tip pen, scissors, paper towels

Piece of medium-weight green cardboard 17 by 17 inches (43 by 43cm)

Double-sided tape, 2 inches (5cm) wide

Heart stencil (page 102)

Craft foam or close-textured synthetic household sponge 2¹⁄₂ by 2¹⁄₂ inches (6.5 by 6.5cm)

Block of wood 2¹⁄₂ by 2¹⁄₂ inches (6.5 by 6.5cm)

Gold craft paint

Saucer, to use as palette

Small craft paint roller (optional)

2 yards (2m) checked ribbon, 1¹⁄₂ inches (4cm) wide

Tissue paper, for lining the box

GIFT: Heart-shaped harvest wreath

1 Arrange the eucalyptus leaves, blueberries, nuts, litchis and cones in groups on a work surface so that they are easy to pick up.

3 Squeeze some glue on the nuts and place them between and over the blueberry and eucalyptus stems. Glue small nuts in clusters and position large nuts individually. Take care to keep within the outlines of the heart shape.

2 Beginning at the top center of the wreath, glue on short sprays of dried blueberries and eucalyptus leaves at intervals around the wreath. Arrange them in varied directions to give the wreath "movement."

4 Glue on litchis where their contrasting color and texture will have maximum effect. They will dry naturally on the wreath. ▶

GIFTWRAP: Forest green and gold box

A simple golden heart shape stamped around the sides of the box echoes the shape of the gift it contains.

5 Add single cones and clusters of small cones, positioning them to face in opposite directions. Glue some of the smaller cones on top of other decorations to enhance the texture contrasts of the wreath.

1 Check the measurements of the completed wreath and adjust the size of the box, if necessary. To make the box shown here, draw on the piece of green cardboard a line 2¹/₂ inches (6.5cm) in from each of the four sides. This measurement represents the depth of the box. The drawn inner square is the base of the box.

2 With the craft knife, lightly score along all the pencil lines, taking care not to cut right through the cardboard.

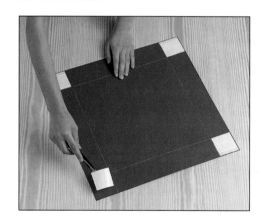

6 Add a few more eucalyptus leaves if you wish, to balance the color around the wreath and to fill in any gaps. ▪

3 Measure and cut strips of double-sided tape to cover each of the squares at the corners. With the scored side uppermost, stick the strips of tape in place. Cut through one of the two lines at each corner.

4 To make the stamp, trace the heart outline on page 102 onto tracing paper and cut it out. Place the heart shape on the foam and draw around it with a felt-tip pen. Cut out the heart-shaped foam and glue it onto the block of wood. Let the glue dry.

5 Pour a little gold paint into the saucer, coat the roller thoroughly, and roll the paint onto the stamp. If you are not using a roller, press the stamp into the paint. Dab off any excess paint with a paper towel.

6 Press the stamp firmly on the outer edges of the cardboard, which will form the sides of the box. Reapply the paint between stampings and repeat the design on all four sides.

7 When the paint is dry, turn the cardboard over and bend along the scored lines to form the box. To make each corner, peel the backing strip from the tape, overlap the cut section and the side of the box, and press together to form a neat, square corner.

8 Cut off 48 inches (1.2m) of the ribbon and trim the edges to neaten them. Wrap the ribbon over one corner of the box, under the next one, over the third corner, and under the fourth. Secure both ends of the ribbon under the box with double-sided tape.

9 Tie the remaining ribbon in a bow, trim the edges, and stick it to the ribbon band with glue or double-sided tape. Line the box with crumpled tissue paper and carefully slide the wreath into the box. 🎁

TABLE-TOP CRANBERRY TREE

AN ELEGANT SILVER PYRAMID-SHAPED BOX opens to reveal a bright and unusual
decoration – a cone-shaped miniature tree laden with fresh cranberries.

GIFT NEEDS

All-purpose glue, craft knife

Piece of modeling clay, about the size of a golf ball

Thick cinnamon stick, or 2 thin sticks, about 5 1/2 inches (14cm) long

Terra-cotta flowerpot 3 1/2 inches (9cm) in diameter and 2 1/2 inches (6.5cm) high

8–10 stones, to weight the pot

Cone-shaped dry floral foam 2 1/2 inches (6.5cm) in diameter and 6 1/2 inches (16.5cm) long, or cut a larger cone to size

About 8 ounces (250g) fresh cranberries or about 6 ounces (175g) dried cranberries

Pack of pearl-headed pins

About 12 fresh bay leaves

1/2 yard (45cm) satin ribbon, 1/8 inch (3mm) wide

Dry sphagnum moss

PACKAGING NEEDS

Ruler, pencil, craft knife, cutting mat

Piece of heavy-weight silver cardboard 12 by 24 inches (30 by 60cm)

1 3/4 yards (1.6m) blue ribbon, 1/8 inch (3mm) wide

White craft glue

Purple paper 12 by 24 inches (30 by 60cm), to line the box

Drawing compass

Large silver bead

GIFT: Table-top cranberry tree

1 Work the piece of modeling clay into a ball and press the cinnamon stick firmly into it. Taking care not to break the cinnamon, press the clay around the stick. Then press the clay into the base of the flowerpot. Glue some stones to the inside of the flowerpot to add weight.

2 Use the pointed end of a craft knife to scoop out a small hole in the center of the base of the cone. This is where the cinnamon trunk will be pressed in to support the tree.

3 If you are using fresh cranberries, spear each one with a pin and, starting at the top of the cone, pin them to the foam close together in rings. Continue until the cone is covered.

4 If you are using dried cranberries, glue on the cranberries in neat rows from the top to the base of one section of the cone. When the glue is dry, turn the cone slightly and glue on more rows of cranberries. Continue until the cone is covered in cranberries. ▶

5 Carefully press the cone onto the cinnamon stick. Pin or glue some bay leaves under the base of the cone to provide color and texture variation.

6 Tie the ribbon in a bow around the rim of the pot. You may need to use a drop of glue to hold the ribbon in place. Alternatively, spiral the ribbon around the tree (right). Cover the top of the pot with moss. ▪▪

GIFTWRAP: Silver pyramid box

This decorative box is square at the base, then takes on a narrow, pyramid shape to follow the lines of the cranberry tree.

1 From the silver cardboard, cut out four rectangles 4½ by 11 inches (11.5 by 28cm) and two squares 5½ by 5½ inches (14 by 14cm). To make the sides, place the rectangles wrong side up.

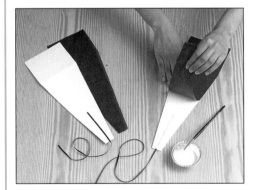

3 Cut the ribbon into four. Glue 4 inches (10cm) down the center of the narrow end of the cardboard on the wrong side. Cut the purple paper to fit and stick it down. Alternatively, glue the paper down first, then trim it to fit.

2 Draw a line 3½ inches (9cm) in from one short side of a rectangle. Score lightly along the line. On the other short side, mark points 1¾ inches (4.5cm) in from each long side. Draw a line from each point to the scored line, then cut off the two triangles. Repeat on the other three rectangles.

4 On the right side of the squares lightly draw and score lines ½ inch (1.5cm) in from all the edges. Draw diagonal lines across the corners, through the intersecting lines, and cut them off.

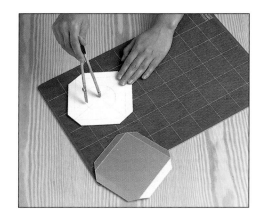

5 To make the inner support piece, draw a circle in the center of one square with a compass. The circle should be large enough for the rim of the pot to rest on it. To calculate the size of the circumference of the circle, measure below the rim of the pot with string. Cut out the circle with a craft knife.

6 To make the base of the box, fold along the scored lines of the other square. Glue purple paper to the wrong side, then trim it to fit with scissors.

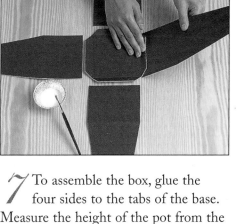

7 To assemble the box, glue the four sides to the tabs of the base. Measure the height of the pot from the base to under the rim. Then, measuring from the bottom of the box, mark this distance on all the sides.

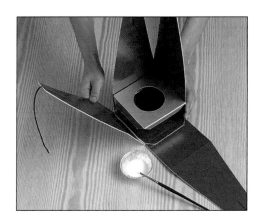

8 Fold the four tabs down and place the inner support piece at the marked height. Check that the pot will fit. Glue two sides of the box to the tabs of the support piece. When the glue has dried, glue the other two sides.

9 Place the cranberry tree gently into the box, taking care not to squash the fresh cranberries.

10 Pull up the sides of the box and thread the ribbons through the silver bead. With two lengths of ribbon in each hand, tie the ribbons in a bow. 🎁

VEGETABLE TABLE WREATH

TELL YOUR HOST OR HOSTESS you will be bringing this colorful, fresh decoration
when you visit, so it can be plced in the center the table at the last minute.

GIFT NEEDS

Scissors

A selection of fresh young vegetables, such as 12–15 snow peas, 10 scallions, 8–12 asparagus, 8–12 baby corn, about 10 radishes, 12 baby carrots, 3-4 chestnut mushrooms, 1–2 bulbs of garlic, 20-25 chilies with stalks

2–3 short sprays of evergreen herbs such as rosemary, sage, or bay (optional)

Raffia

About 20 floral wires

Wire cutters

Straw wreath form, 8 inches (20cm) in diameter

PACKAGING NEEDS

Slatted wood basket or tray 12 inches (30cm) in diameter and 4 inches (10cm) high

Fine-grit sandpaper (optional)

Soft cloth (optional)

Red and green acrylic water-based paints

2 foil containers, to use as palettes

Small paintbrush

Tissue paper, for lining basket

1 yard (1m) wire-edged taffeta ribbon, 1 inch (2.5cm) wide (optional)

1-2 floral wires (optional)

GIFT: Vegetable table wreath

Keep all the vegetables in the refrigerator until you are ready to compose the wreath.

1 Remove all the vegetables from the refrigerator and sort them into their separate groups. Discard any vegetables that are damaged or discolored.

3 Make a small bundle of baby corn, with roughly half the heads facing in each direction. Tie the bundle with raffia, as in Step 2.

2 Gather six or eight snow peas, and shape them into a bundle. Bind a strand of raffia around them a couple of times, tie it in a knot, and cut off the loose ends with scissors.

4 Tie the stalks of the chilies together with raffia just above the tops of the vegetables. Make bundles of other vegetables, such as scallions, asparagus, and carrots. Use cocktail sticks to spear the radishes. ▶

5 Add variety to the wreath by using small individual vegetables such as turnips, beets, bulbs of garlic, or mushrooms. To make stems for them, cut a floral wire in half and push it through the vegetable. Twist the two ends of the wire together to form a single stem which you will be able to push into the wreath form.

6 To attach the vegetable bundles to the wreath, cut a floral wire in half, thread it through the raffia at the back of the bundle, and twist the ends together. Push the wires almost horizontally into the wreath.

7 Compose the decoration by placing the bundles and individual vegetables in a single layer over the wreath form, alternating the color and texture as much as possible. Check that the vegetables are held firmly in place.

8 Twirl some strands of raffia together, tie a bow, and tease out the strands. Push a wire through the back of the bow and press the wire into the wreath.

9 If you wish, tuck sprigs of herbs, such as sage and rosemary, between the vegetables to add a refreshing aroma. Keep the wreath refrigerated until the last moment. ■■

GIFTWRAP: Zigzag basket

The slatted basket, painted in scarlet and green, will protect the wreath
en route to a party, and be useful later to hold rolls or cheese.

1 Rub the basket with fine sandpaper if necessary, then dust it with a soft cloth. Paint the rim and base strip with red paint, then leave to dry. Apply a second coat if necessary.

2 The pattern on the basket is made by painting zigzag strips of slats in red, and filling the spaces between them in green. As a guide, dab a spot of red paint on the relevant squares.

3 Paint the red squares and leave the paint to dry. Apply a second coat of paint if necessary. Then paint the rest of the squares green.

4 When the basket is dry, paint the handles with green paint, taking great care not to go over the red edges. Let it dry and apply a second coat of paint if necessary.

5 Line the basket with crumpled tissue paper and lay the wreath on top. If you wish, make one or two bows with wire-edged ribbon and attach them to one or both of the handles with floral wire. 🎁

Note

Give your wreath a professional finish by brushing over the vegetable bundles with oil until the

wreath glistens. Take care not to get oil on the raffia bow.

NATURAL TREE DECORATIONS

RINGS OF GOLDEN KUMQUATS AND CHILIES and clusters of miniature pomanders
make eye-catching tree decorations, presented in a gold-speckled box.

GIFT NEEDS

Scissors, felt-tip pen

About 2¹/₂ yards (2.5m) green, plastic-covered flexible wire

Wire cutters

About 30 kumquats

6 each red and green chilies

5 each red and yellow round (Scotch bonnet) chilies

3¹/₂ yards (3.5m) gold metallic ribbon, 1 inch (2.5cm) wide

About 3 tablespoons of whole cloves

Box of short gold-headed pins

2 yards (2m) gold metallic ribbon, ¹/₈ inch (3mm) wide

2 cinnamon sticks

Needle and yellow thread

Makes 2 kumquat rings, 4 chili rings, and 2 kumquat pomanders

PACKAGING NEEDS

Wooden cheese box base, about 14 inches (35cm) in diameter and 2 inches (5cm) high

Fine-grit sandpaper (optional)

Soft cloth (optional)

Orange acrylic water-based paint

Gold acrylic paint

Small foil containers, to use as palettes

2 small paintbrushes

Clear water-based varnish

1 or 2 short branches of spruce or other evergreen tree

Shears or floral scissors

5 inches (12.5cm) thin-gauge flexible wire

1 yard (1m) wire-edged multicolored ribbon, 2¹/₄ inches (5.5cm) wide

GIFT: Natural tree decorations
Wash your hands after handling the chilies to avoid skin irritation.

1 To make each kumquat ring, select about 8 or 10 fruits of roughly equal size. Using wire cutters, cut 12 inches (30cm) flexible wire and thread the fruits on it, leaving 2 inches (5cm) of wire free at each end.

2 Join the ring by twisting the two ends of wire neatly around each other. This will leave a gap at the top of the ring for a bow.

3 Cut about 17 inches (42.5cm) of the wide ribbon and trim the ends into a V shape with scissors. Tie the ribbon in a bow at the top of the ring. Ease out the loops to cover the wire.

4 To make a chili ring, select five or six red and green chilies, depending on size, and thread them on a 12-inch (30-cm) length of wire, alternating the colors. Join the ring as described in Step 2 and decorate it with a bow as described in Step 3. Do the same with the round chilies. ▶

5 To make each kumquat pomander, cut three pieces of flexible wire, each 2 inches (5cm) long. Bend them to a U shape and push the ends of each one into the stalk end of a fruit, leaving a small loop protruding.

6 Before decorating the kumquats, draw guidelines around each fruit to indicate longitudinal, horizontal, or spiral guidelines around it.

7 Following the drawn lines, press whole cloves into the fruit leaving a small space between cloves for the gold-headed pins.

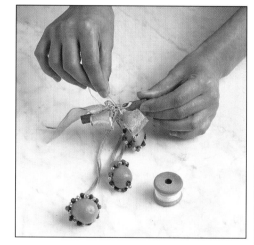

8 To add some sparkle to the decoration, press gold-headed pins into the kumquats in the spaces between the cloves. Decorate the other two kumquats in a similar way.

9 Cut three pieces of the narrow ribbon, 8, 12, and 16 inches (20, 30, and 40cm) long respectively. Thread one end of a piece of ribbon through the wire loop at the top of one of the kumquats. Tie and knot the ends of the ribbon together. Thread and tie the other two ribbons to the other kumquats in the same way.

10 Cut 12 inches (30cm) of the wide ribbon, and tie it in a bow around a cinnamon stick. Turn under about ¼ inch (6mm) of the free ends of each of the narrow ribbons and sew them to the back of the ribbon bow so the kumquats hang in a cluster. ▪

GIFTWRAP: Branching out

Present a selection of fruit and vegetable Christmas tree decorations the way they will be displayed, on evergreen branches.

1 Sand the box base if necessary, then dust it with a soft cloth. Pour some orange paint in a container and paint the box inside and out. Let it dry and apply a second coat if needed, and let it dry again.

2 To spatter the box with gold, pour a little gold paint into a container and dip the tip of the brush into it. Hold the brush firmly in one hand and use the index finger of your other hand to flick the bristles. Alternatively, tap the brush against your finger.

3 Spatter the box both inside and out with gold paint. When the paint is thoroughly dry, varnish the box to protect the painted surface.

4 Trim the evergreen branches with shears or floral scissors so they fit in the box. Attach the decorations to the branches with short lengths of wire.

5 Tie the multicolored ribbon in a bow and neaten the ends. Thread the wire through the bow and attach it to a branch at the back of the box. 🎁

Note

Leave the ends of the branches hanging casually over the edge of the box or for a more formal look, tuck them in neatly (see page 112.)

SQUASH CANDLE LAMPS

CARVE OUT SIMPLE STAR AND MOON SHAPES from a selection of hollowed-out squash to make a stylish group of Thanksgiving candleholders.

GIFT NEEDS

Thin-bladed kitchen knife, dessert spoon, craft knife or scissors, tracing paper, felt-tip pen, pencil

Selection of 4–6 small squash or pumpkins

Selection of small cookie cutters or star and moon stencils (page 118)

4–6 tea light candles

PACKAGING NEEDS

Tracing paper, felt-tip pen, cutting mat, craft knife, masking tape, paper towels

Wooden basket with handle 8¹/₂ by 13 inches (21.5 by 33cm)

Fine-grit sandpaper

Soft cloth

Blue-green acrylic water-based paint

Small foil container, to use as palette

Paintbrush

Cornucopia stencil (page 118)

Sheet of plain paper

Brown, green, orange, and purple dry-brush oil-based stencil paints

Scrap of cardboard

Stencil brush

Clear water-based varnish

Small paintbrush

Chopped straw, for packing

GIFT: Squash candle lamps

1 With a kitchen knife, cut off the top of each squash. If the vegetable narrows at the top, check that it will be wide enough for the candle once it has been hollowed out. If not, cut it lower down, at a wider part. Reserve the "lid" sections.

2 Using a spoon, scoop out the flesh and seeds from the center of each squash, taking care to leave firm walls.

3 Cut out small pieces of tracing paper and draw around the star- and moon-shaped cookie cutters. Alternatively, trace the pattern for the star and moon shapes on page 118 or draw shapes of your own. Cut out the shapes to use as templates.

4 Place one of the templates on the side and toward the top of the first squash. Ideally, when the shapes are cut out, the candlelight should shine through the openings without the base of the candle being visible. Draw around the shape with a pencil. ▶

5 Hold the kitchen knife on the pencil outline with the blade at a right angle to the side of the squash and press the point into the skin. Cut around the shape with sawing movements and remove the cutout section. With the knife at the same angle, clean up the edges of the opening.

6 Position the star and moon templates around the squash and cut out the shapes as before. Take care not to cut out shapes too close together as this will weaken the walls of the squash.

7 Repeat the tracing and cutting out of shapes on the other squash. You can vary the patterns and the shapes; choose ones that will not be too difficult to cut around.

8 Check that each squash will stand straight. If not, cut a thin sliver from the base to level it. Place a tea light candle inside the squash and replace the cut-off lid sections. ▪▪

GIFTWRAP: Thanksgiving basket

A wooden basket stenciled with a cornucopia design takes its theme from the rich tradition of Thanksgiving.

1 Sand the basket and dust it with a soft cloth. Pour a little blue-green paint into a foil container, dilute it with water, and mix thoroughly. Brush the paint over the basket, staining it lightly.

2 Draw around the outline of the cornucopia on tracing paper and use a craft knife to cut out the outline. Experiment with the colors you would like to use on a sheet of paper first. We used brown for the basket, green for the leaves, orange and purple for the fruits.

3 Position the stencil on one side of the basket and anchor it with masking tape. Rub a little of the first color on a scrap of cardboard and pick up the color on a stencil brush. Dab off any excess paint on paper towel. By dabbing the brush into first one color and then another, you can blend the colors on the brush.

4 Color in the rest of the stencil, taking care not to smudge the paint. Remove the stencil and clean it with paper towels. Reverse the stencil, position it next to the first pattern, and color it the same way.

5 Stencil all around the basket and let it dry. Apply varnish to the basket and let it dry before packing it with chopped straw and arranging the squash on top. 🎁

Note

Instead of using a wooden basket, you could present the squash candle lamps in a wooden, cardboard, or papier-mâché box, painting and stenciling it in a similar way.

PLACE SETTING POMANDERS

A SET OF CITRUS FRUIT POMANDERS, EACH ONE OUTLINED with the initial letter of everyone in the family, provides a novel and practical place indicator for a family dinner party.

GIFT NEEDS

*Pencil, tracing paper, paper towel,
masking tape*

3 small lemons

3 limes

4-5 tablespoons whole cloves

Fine skewer or darning needle

Blue tack

*6 wooden napkin rings or
mini flowerpots*

PACKAGING NEEDS

*Paper towel, scissors, all-purpose glue or
double-sided tape, 2 tall jars or cans*

*Round wooden, cardboard or papier-mâché
box at least 7½ inches (19cm) in diameter
and 4 inches (10cm) deep*

*Blue, bright yellow, and lemon yellow
acrylic water-based paints*

Small paintbrush

3 small foil containers, to use as palettes

Clear water-based flat varnish

Hot pink tissue paper, for packing

*1 yard (1m) each sheer ribbon,
1½ inches (4cm) wide in lemon and lime*

GIFT: Place setting pomanders

*The pomanders can be made up to one day in advance. After the
occasion, the fruit will dry out naturally for a lasting memento.*

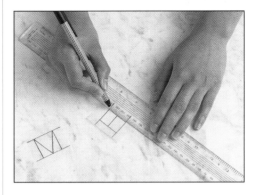

1 On pieces of tracing paper, draw
the outlines of the letters of the
alphabet you will need for your place
names. To keep the letters the same size,
draw the letters between two ruled lines
about 1 to 1½ inches (2.5cm) apart,
depending on the size of the fruit.

3 Remove the paper and draw over
the outline of the letter with a
felt-tip pen to increase the definition.
Press cloves close together into the
skin, piercing more holes if necessary.

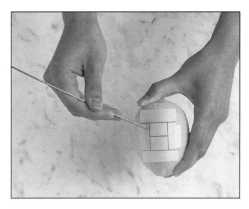

2 Secure the outline of one of the
letters just above the center of
one lemon with some masking tape.
Prick through the outline with a
skewer. These holes will also make it
easier to press in the cloves. Wipe off
any juice that oozes out of the fruit
with paper towel.

4 Transfer the letter outlines to the
other lemons and limes and fill in
the letters with cloves. ▶

5 With the skewer, pierce a ring of holes around the top of each fruit, wiping any juice away with paper towels. Press cloves close together to form a complete circle.

6 Secure each fruit to the napkin ring by either pressing a piece of Blue tack into each ring, or by placing two small pieces on the rim of each ring. Press one of the fruits onto each napkin ring, checking that the fruit is held firmly in place. ▪

GIFTWRAP: Citrus-colored box

Like the fruits inside, this citrus-yellow box is dramatically contrasted with vivid blue and decorated with a lemon-lime bow.

1 Place the box lid on one of the jars and paint the lid blue. Leave it to dry, then apply a second coat if necessary. Wash the paintbrush.

3 When the lid and the box are dry, paint the insides with blue paint. Take care at the rim of the box base not to spoil the line of yellow paint.

2 Place the box base upside-down on the other jar and paint it bright yellow. When it is dry, apply a second coat if necessary.

4 Pour a little of the lemon yellow paint into a small container and dilute it with a little water. Mix thoroughly with a clean paintbrush.

5 Put a little of the diluted lemon yellow paint on the brush and wipe off any excess on paper towels. Using light brush strokes, paint quickly over the box base in the same direction to give a streaked effect.

6 When the paint is dry, brush over the box and lid with varnish to seal the painted surfaces. Leave the varnish to dry. If you wish, apply a second coat.

7 Crumple the sheets of hot pink tissue paper and line the box with them. Carefully arrange the pomanders in the box, taking care not to dislodge them from their rings.

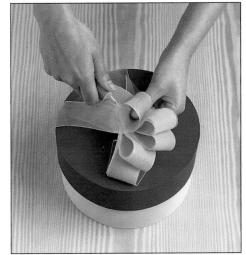

8 Hold the two lengths of ribbon together and make a small loop in one hand. Continue making four or five small loops, holding the end of each loop under your thumb. Secure the loops by stapling them together or sewing a few stitches in the middle.

9 Stick the bow to the box with glue or double-sided tape and trim the ends neatly. ✤

Note

Check with the recipient which initial letters of family and friends will be appropriate for your "place cards" gift.

HOLIDAY TABLE ARRANGEMENT

EVERGREEN LEAVES AND SMALL FRUITS glistening with silver
and gold make a festive centerpiece for any party table.

GIFT NEEDS

Scissors, floral scissors, baking sheet, waxed paper

About 4 ounces (125g) green grapes

1 small egg white, lightly beaten

2 tablespoons (30ml) superfine sugar

5-6 short sprays of evergreen leaves such as bay, juniper, and rosemary

Cylinder of absorbent floral foam, 3½ inches (9cm) in diameter

Plastic holder 6 inches (15cm) in diameter, for floral foam

Piece of plastic-covered wire net about 10 by 10 inches (25 by 25cm)

Florist tape

15-20 medium floral wires

Wire cutters

3 small apples

3-5 each passion fruit and litchis

Gold craft paste and paintbrush

Water-based size or wallpaper paste

2 sheets silver leaf

Piece of plain paper

PACKAGING NEEDS

Ruler, pencil, scissors, cutting mat, craft knife

Round cardboard or papier-mâché box at least 10 inches (25cm) in diameter and 5 inches (12.5cm) high

Gold wrapping paper, to cover box

Double-sided tape, 2 inches (5cm) wide

Water-based size or wallpaper paste

5-6 sheets of gold-colored metal leaf

2 yards (2m) sheer ribbon, 1½ inches (4cm) wide

2-3 sprays evergreen leaves, to decorate lid

Tissue paper, to line box

GIFT: Holiday table arrangement

Make frosted grapes the day before you want to use them, since this gives them enough time to dry.

1 Cut the grapes into small clusters. Dip the fruit in the lightly beaten egg white, then sprinkle over the sugar so that the fruit is completely covered. Place the clusters on a baking sheet lined with waxed paper and leave in a warm, dry place overnight.

3 To give each apple a false stem, push a floral wire through the fruit close to the base, cross over the ends and twist them together. Wire the passion fruit and litchis the same way.

2 Put the foliage in water and soak the floral foam until saturated. Put the foam into the plastic holder, crumple up the wire net, and press it over the foam. Hold everything in place with two strips of florist tape at right angles. Stick the ends to the holder.

4 Brush the apples with gold craft paste, leaving a few small areas uncovered. To attach the silver leaf, mix a little size according to the product instructions and brush it in small patches over the gilded apples. ▶

5 Tear small pieces from the sheets of silver leaf. Drop the pieces on the pasted areas on the fruit and smooth them by patting them with a piece of paper. Gently rub the apples with a finger to give them a distressed look.

6 Brush the wired passion fruit and litchis with gold craft paste, allowing the color of the fruit to show through in some small areas.

7 Remove the evergreen stems from water and cut them 5 to 6 inches (12.5 to 15cm) long with floral scissors. Arrange the leaves around the base of the floral foam to hide it, then add more leaves to make a rounded shape.

Note

The litchis and passion fruit will dry successfully on the arrangement, but the apples may need to be replaced when they become soft and wrinkled. Alternatively, fill the space left by the apples with evergreen leaves.

8 Arrange the apples evenly around the arrangement so that their weight is evenly balanced. Arrange the passion fruit and litchis among the leaves, positioning some to hang over the container rim.

9 Wrap wires around the grape stems and arrange them among the other fruits. Turn the decoration around, check that it is equally attractive from all angles, and fill in any gaps with more leaves. ▪▪

GIFTWRAP: Shimmering with gold

A round box covered with gold paper is decorated with gold-colored leaf, trimmed with gossamer ribbon and finished off with a spray of evergreen.

1 Cover the box and lid with gold wrapping paper, as described in the instructions on pages 34 and 35.

2 Mix some sizing or wallpaper paste and brush it in patches randomly over the side of the box. Tear off small pieces of gold-colored leaf and drop them on the pasted areas.

3 Place a small piece of plain paper over the patches of gold leaf and pat them down. Do not rub the paper over the gold as the gold leaf may break off, but do not worry if the gold leaf wrinkles. Continue adding scraps of gold leaf around the sides of the box and to the top of the lid, and pat them down with paper.

4 Cut off 1½ yards (1.5m) of ribbon. Cut about six ¾-inch (1.5 -cm) strips of double-sided tape and stick them at intervals around the side of the lid. Peel off the backing paper, press the ribbon onto one of the strips, and pull it taut around the lid. Press the ribbon on to the other strips of tape. Tie in a bow and trim the ends.

5 To decorate the lid, gather some foliage sprays together and tie the remaining ribbon around them in a bow. Attach the decoration to the lid with double-sided tape. Line the box with tissue paper and carefully put the arrangement inside. ✿

Note

Crafter's "gold" leaf is actually made from a gold-colored metal-alloy pressed into very thin sheets. When using gold leaf, always pick it up with a small paintbrush – if you touch it, it will stick to your skin.

INDEX

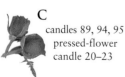
ACKNOWLEDGMENTS
The author and publishers are grateful to the
following individuals and companies for their
assistance in compiling this book: **Phil Gamble**
for drawing all the stencil outlines; **Michele
Grigoletti** for scanning assistance; **Caroline
Brooke-Johnson** for the index; C M Offray &
Son for providing the ribbons used to decorate
the packages throughout the book. A special
thanks to **Iain Bagwell** for the use of his
backgrounds. The author would also like
to thank Esther Labi, Helen Spencer
and Andrew Sydenham for all their
effort and hard work.